JOHN 1-12
FOR YOU

JOSH MOODY
JOHN 1-12
FOR YOU

thegoodbook
COMPANY

John 1–12 For You

© Josh Moody/The Good Book Company, 2017

Published by:
The Good Book Company

Tel (US): 866 244 2165
Tel (UK): 0333 123 0880
Email (US): info@thegoodbook.com
Email (UK): info@thegoodbook.co.uk

Websites:

North America: www.thegoodbook.com
UK: www.thegoodbook.co.uk
Australia: www.thegoodbook.com.au
New Zealand: www.thegoodbook.co.nz

(Hardcover) ISBN: 9781784982164
(Paperback) ISBN: 9781784982157

Design by André Parker

Printed in India

CONTENTS

SERIES PREFACE

Each volume of the *God's Word For You* series takes you to the heart of a book of the Bible, and applies its truths to your heart.

The central aim of each title is to be:

- ■ Bible centered
- ■ Christ glorifying
- ■ Relevantly applied
- ■ Easily readable

You can use *John 1–12 For You:*

To read. You can simply read from cover to cover, as a book that explains and explores the themes, encouragements and challenges of this part of Scripture.

To feed. You can work through this book as part of your own personal regular devotions, or use it alongside a sermon or Bible-study series at your church. Each chapter is divided into two (or occasionally three) shorter sections, with questions for reflection at the end of each.

To lead. You can use this as a resource to help you teach God's word to others, both in small-group and whole-church settings. You'll find tricky verses or concepts explained using ordinary language, and helpful themes and illustrations along with suggested applications.

These books are not commentaries. They assume no understanding of the original Bible languages, nor a high level of biblical knowledge. Verse references are marked in **bold** so that you can refer to them easily. Any words that are used rarely or differently in everyday language outside the church are marked in gray when they first appear, and are explained in a glossary toward the back. There, you'll also find details of resources you can use alongside this one, in both personal and church life.

Our prayer is that as you read, you'll be struck not by the contents of this book, but by the book it's helping you open up; and that you'll praise not the author of this book, but the One he is pointing you to.

Carl Laferton, Series Editor

FOREWORD

Someone once said that John's Gospel is "deep enough for an elephant to swim and shallow enough for a child not to drown." I've never been able to conclusively verify the source of the saying (though many attribute it to Augustine), but there's a reason why this quote is so popular: it captures a profound truth about John's Gospel.

On the one hand, learned commentaries and **theological treatises*** have been written over the centuries, grappling with the sublime theological insights embedded in John's deceptively simple language. On the other hand, every child knows (or at least used to know) passages such as John 3:16: "God so loved the world that he gave his one and only Son, that whoever believes in him shall not perish but have eternal life." And when a new Christian asks me where he should start reading the Bible, I generally recommend that he or she start with the Gospel of John.

John's Gospel is a **literary** and theological masterpiece. As the final Gospel to be written and included in the **canon** of Scripture, it climaxes the New Testament's account of the life, death, resurrection, and exaltation of Jesus and the salvation he came to bring. The ending of the Gospel—"This is the disciple who testifies to these things and who wrote them down. We know that his testimony is true. Jesus did many other things as well. If every one of them were written down, I suppose that even the whole world would not have room for the books that would be written" (21:24–25)—concludes not only John's Gospel but the fourfold Gospel with which the New Testament begins.

From the **Prologue** to the **Epilogue**, John's Gospel reveals careful literary composition and theological **exposition**. In the Prologue, the author—John the **apostle**, the son of Zebedee, one of the Twelve and Jesus' closest follower during his earthly ministry—sets the stage for his magnificent drama of the Word become flesh, who

---

* Words in **gray** are defined in the Glossary (page 209).

took up temporary residence among us and revealed the Father definitively in both word and deed, and supremely in his cross-death and subsequent resurrection. In this Word—the Lord Jesus Christ— God effected a new creation of which Jesus' disciples served as the first representatives.

Then, John casts the drama of God's sent Son in the form of two major acts: The Book of Signs (chapters 1 – 12) and The Book of Exaltation, or Glory (chapters 13 – 21). In the first act, Jesus is shown to reveal himself to God's people, Israel, during the course of two major ministry cycles—the Cana Cycle (chapters 2 – 4) and the Festival Cycle (chapters 5 – 10). John's account of Jesus' seven **messianic signs** culminates in the narrative of the matchless raising of Lazarus (chapters 11 – 12), by which Jesus reveals himself as "the resurrection and the life," and signals that he himself will soon rise from the dead.

The second act, remarkably, adopts the vantage point of Jesus' exaltation with God in heaven. From John's vantage point, Jesus' finished cross-work is a **fait accompli**: "It is finished" (19:30). Thus, Jesus shows his disciples the full extent of his love, **incipiently** at the footwashing and climactically at the foot of the cross. Three days later, Jesus appears to his followers a total of three times, and **commissions** them as his representatives to take the gospel of salvation to the unbelieving world: "As the Father has sent me, so I am sending you" (20:21).

Indeed, even the feet of an elephant swimming in John's Gospel wouldn't touch the bottom, so deep and rich is its theology. And yet, every child can read the story of, say, Nicodemus, the teacher of Israel, and learn that he or she must be born again. To be sure, a child may not understand exactly what being "born again" means, but he or she will be able to relate to the illustration of the wind, whose origins are unknown but whose effects can be observed, and catch a glimpse of the spiritual transformation that is required for anyone to be able to enter the presence of the holy and righteous God when they die.

Now, because John's Gospel is so deep and yet so simple, there's a need not only for academic commentaries but also for accessible, spiritually sensitive treatments and reflections. Josh Moody has given us a stimulating and edifying exemplar of the latter. He hasn't merely reported or repeated what John's Gospel says; rather, he has creatively processed John's teaching and relates it consistently and faithfully to people living in the real world today. As a **Johannine scholar**, I greatly welcome this because when writing academic works on the Gospel, there's often little room for the much-needed application.

My invitation for you, therefore, is simple, echoing another (more easily verifiable!) quote by Augustine: *"Tolle, lege!"*—take up and read! Read this volume, and yet, as you do so, don't forget to read also the Gospel which is so capably elucidated in the pages of the book you're about to enjoy.

Dr Andreas J. Köstenberger

Founder, Biblical Foundations™ (www.biblicalfoundations.org)
Senior Research Professor of New Testament and Biblical Theology,
Southeastern Baptist Theological Seminary

Bible translations used:

- NIV: New International Version, 2011 translation (This is the version being quoted unless otherwise stated.)

- NIV84: New International Version, 1984 translation

- ESV: English Standard Version

- NLT: New Living Translation

INTRODUCTION TO JOHN 1 - 12

John's Gospel is an invitation to you to find life.

The standard structure of John's Gospel, which Andreas Köstenberger so ably and excellently outlines for us in his foreword on page 9, is one that I follow throughout this and the next volume. Within that framework, it is typical to regard John 20:30-31 as the apostle John's definitive statement as to the purpose of his writing his book:

> "Jesus performed many other signs in the presence of his disciples, which are not recorded in this book. But these are written that you may believe that Jesus is the Messiah*, the Son of God, and that by believing you may have life in his name."

I will leave the explanation of these crucial verses to the appropriate place in that second volume of this guide. But it is important here, in the introduction to this first volume, to indicate our general trajectory, so that the various details that will be explained in this volume can begin to fit coherently into a whole in our minds.

First of all, the "signs" that John describes (which are covered in the first volume) are for a particular purpose; namely, that we may "believe that Jesus is the Messiah, the Son of God, and that by believing [we] may have life in his name." That statement, while on the surface fairly clear, does raise multiple other related questions of interpretation, and therefore also of application. For instance, what does it mean to "believe"? What sort of "life" is it that we have through belief in Jesus and in his name? And is this "belief" in Jesus meant to indicate to us that John's Gospel is primarily evangelistic in orientation?

As I say, I will leave the precise exegesis of that passage to the appropriate place in the second volume, but at this point I need to say the following. It seems to me clear that John does not only have in mind "evangelism" (that is, verbal outreach to those who are not yet saved), nor does he only have in mind "discipleship" (encouraging

---

* Words in gray are defined in the Glossary (page 209).

those who are already Christians to grow in their relationship with God and their obedience to him). Instead, because John is both at one level so simple—so appropriate for those just beginning to explore the Christian faith—and also at another level so profound, John's Gospel seems to me to be intended to operate at both levels throughout. It is written both for the "seeker" and for the "disciple."

The key in some ways is not so much the word "believe" or the concept of faith (which John will explain throughout his book, both by monologue and by narrative), but that word "life." The great twentieth-century preacher D. Martyn Lloyd-Jones thought that the key to understanding and appreciating John's Gospel was not John 20, but (surprisingly for many modern scholars) the beginning of John's Gospel—what we call his Prologue (1:1-18). Lloyd-Jones thought that in his letters (1, 2, and 3 John), the

> The key is not so much the word "believe" but that word "life."

apostle John typically indicated his purpose and point at the beginning of his writing, and that he did the same in John's Gospel. For him, John's Gospel was about showing us how to have this "life" (1:4)—"life to the full" in Jesus' name (10:10). The discourse with the woman at the well in John chapter 4 was particularly important for Lloyd-Jones as an illustration of that theme in John; for instance:

> "Whoever drinks the water I give them will never thirst. Indeed, the water I give them will become in them a spring of water welling up to eternal life." (John 4:13-14)

So it is my prayer, as you read this first volume of this guide to John, that you would not simply have a deeper understanding of the text (though I certainly hope that is the case), nor simply have a list of practical "to-dos" for how to apply the text in a somewhat mechanical fashion (though I certainly hope that such practical application will result), but that you will be drawn to read more and more of John's

Gospel itself, and encounter more and more deeply Jesus, the Christ, the Son of God. It is as you do so that you will find "life" in and with him, with all the wonderful consequences—not least, forgiveness, fulfillment, and freedom—that John's Gospel lays out.

That way, this guide will avoid the trap of dryness that the philosopher and theologian Soren Kierkegaard highlighted when he advised that the first step to church and personal renewal was, "first of all to kill all the **commentators**." In other words, I hope and pray that this book will be a mere lens through which you can examine the Bible itself more closely, and enjoy and magnify the Christ that John's Gospel reveals.

1. THE WORD AND THE WITNESS

Today it is often assumed that the Christian understanding of ultimate matters—the origin of life, the meaning of life, the basic framework that gives explanations to science and reason—is substantially weakened by the discoveries of the scientific consensus over the last hundreds of years. You will often come across someone who says, "I can't believe that, because of science." Or they will say, "That old-fashioned myth about Christianity is simply not credible anymore." If you ever find yourself wondering about the basic truth structure of Christianity, or if you have conversations with people who do, then John, and especially John chapter 1, is for you! Here we discover that the underpinning *logos*, or structure and order of the universe, is all centered on a person. John's logic is persuasive, and his foundational commitment to the truth of God as revealed in Christ is no small superficiality; it is deeper than the ocean.

The fourth-century bishop and theologian Augustine is said to have commented that the Gospel of John is "deep enough for an elephant to swim and shallow enough for a child not to drown." John's "Prologue" is one of the most profound parts of John, but at the same time its message is quite simple. Probably the easiest way to understand its main theme is by comparing the beginning and end of this introduction to John's Gospel. (Note, though, that the division of the first eighteen verses from the rest of John was probably not technically formalized until sometime after 1777, with Griesbach's edition of the Greek New Testament. It is arguable that the **archetype** contained no division at **verse 18***, though it did have one at **verse 5**. This guide maintains the (now) traditional view of John's "Prologue" (meaning the first 18 verses), but examines those verses for the way they also introduce the role of John the Baptist, which is otherwise likely to be viewed as a digression in the argument; his role is further developed after **verse 19**. (For more detail on this point, see P. J. Williams, "Not the Prologue of John," in the *Journal for the Study of the New Testament*.)

In the Beginning

Verse 1 reads, "In the beginning was the Word, and the Word was with God, and the Word was God." **Verse 14a** reads, "The Word became flesh and made his dwelling among us."

John's Prologue, then, at its most simple, is a description of how the Word, which was in the beginning, became flesh. This subject of "the Word" runs throughout the first 18 verses. The scholar D. A. Carson puts it this way:

> "The emphasis of the Prologue … is on the revelation of the Word as the ultimate disclosure of God himself."   (*John*, page 135)

There is one other major aspect of the theme in these verses: the witness. You can see this in the second half of **verse 14** and the beginning of **verse 15**: "We have seen his glory, the glory of the one and only Son … full of **grace** and truth. John testified concerning him…"

Throughout the early verses of John's Gospel, then, you will find two interlocking and interweaving themes that intertwine like two pieces of string: the Word and the witness.

- ■ The Word: **verses 1-5**
- ■ The witness: **verses 6-9**
- ■ The Word: **verses 10-14a**
- ■ The witness: **verses 14b-18**

---

* All John verse references being looked at in each chapter part are in **bold**.

So John's Prologue may be summarized most simply by these two themes of "the Word" and "the witness," along the lines of this one statement: How the Word that was in the beginning became flesh, and how we witnessed to this Word. As Köstenberger writes:

> "In Jesus, God has come to take up residence among his people once again, in a way even more intimate than when he dwelt in the midst of wilderness Israel in the tabernacle. Moses met God and heard his word in the 'tent of meeting'; now people may meet God and hear him in the flesh of Jesus." (John, page 41)

That said, while John's Prologue is indeed "shallow enough for a child not to drown," it is also "deep enough for an elephant to swim." The challenge is to plumb the depths without getting lost or disorientated, or drowning! And the way to do that is to keep in mind the basic message and simple structure of these two intertwining themes of "the Word" and "the witness."

In **verses 1-5** ("the Word"), John tells us of the identity of this Word and his role in creation. When John says that the Word was "in the beginning" (**v 1**), he is referring to the first sentence of the whole Bible, Genesis 1:1: "In the beginning God created..." John is making the remarkable claim that the Word that became flesh is the eternal Word that "was with God in the beginning" (John **1:2**), which was the Word by which God made everything (**v 3**—"And God said..." occurs frequently in Genesis 1), and that was God himself (John **1:1**).

The Greek of the second half of **verse 1** is literally "and God was the Word." The great sixteenth-century **Reformer** Martin Luther believed it should have been translated that way. Today, **Jehovah's Witnesses** think that because there is no definite article ("the" in English) before "God" in that second half of the verse, it should be translated as "the Word was a god." However, the same construction in Greek is used later in verse 49, which is translated by everyone, including the Jehovah's Witnesses, as, "You are the king of Israel" (not a king of Israel). Scholars agree that if John had wanted to write that the Word was fully God, then, literally, "and God was the Word" is how to do it in Greek:

"The force of the *anarthrous* is probably not so much that of definiteness as that of quality: Jesus 'shared the essence of the Father, though they differed in person.'"

(Köstenberger, *John*, page 28)

This Word was "toward" God, literally, suggesting an eternal bond face to face between co-equal Persons enjoying relationship with each other:

"For John, the reason the Son can make the Father known is not only because he was in the bosom of the Father, but because he is also the Word who was in the beginning with God. He is described as God."

(S. Hamid-Khani, *Revelation and Concealment of Christ*, page 356)

As the fourth-century bishop and celebrated preacher Gregory of Nazianzus, nicknamed "Goldentongue," said:

"I cannot think of the One without the Three forthwith shining around me." (Quoted in John Calvin, *Calvin's New Testament Commentaries*, Vol. 1, page 9)

The "Word" in Greek is *logos*, a well-known Greek term that was used by Greek philosophers for the ancient principle that undergirded everything. Most likely, John is using this specific term primarily to reference Genesis 1:1—"In the beginning":

"The Prologue summarizes how the 'Word', which was with God in the very beginning, came into the sphere of time, history, tangibility—in other words, how the Son of God was sent into the world to become the Jesus of history, so that the glory and grace of God might be uniquely and perfectly disclosed"

(D. A. Carson, *John*, page 111)

But John's purpose is also to build a bridge to a **worldview** which believed that there was some eternal principle of *logos* behind everything:

"The scope of Jesus' own **salvific** mission is the whole world. He is the light that shines in the world, enlightening every man by his coming into the world."

(S. Hamid-Khani, *Revelation and Concealment of Christ*, page 172)

Today, too, that kind of **apologetic** for the existence of God is compelling. Atheists are ultimately making the claim that thought, ideas, and immaterial intelligence are generated by matter. This appears unlikely at a rational level: those who demand that there is nothing but matter are using arguments that are nonmaterial. Atheism is arguably a logically self-refuting proposition. John makes the case that the *logos*—the immaterial intelligence which alone can explain rational thought, the laws of science, and the mathematical structure of reality—is actually a Person to whom he witnesses.

> Those who demand there is nothing but matter are using arguments that are nonmaterial.

"The light shines in the darkness, and the darkness has not overcome it" (John **1:5**) is a little opaque. Does John mean the light of salvation or the light of conscience? Does he mean that the darkness has not intellectually understood or has not actually overcome it (the word can have both meanings)? Here we start to explore a facet of John's writing that has infuriated experts and engaged children. John deliberately uses language with intentional depth of meaning. We have to be careful not to read into John all sorts of things that he never intended. But on occasions, we can see that John deliberately envisioned more than one level of meaning with one word. Here, John means that the light of creation, shining in human conscience and the natural order, while damaged by human rebellion after Genesis 3, has not been destroyed, and that the darkness has also not overcome that light.

In the writing of the apostle Paul, in Romans 1:20 and 3:21, we can see a commentary on this verse. Romans 1:20 tells us that "since the creation of the world God's invisible qualities—his eternal power and divine nature—have been clearly seen, being understood from what has been made, so that people are without excuse." God has shown himself in creation: the light shines, and yet the darkness has not understood it or overcome it. There is in creation a light, a light of God, that shines in the darkness, and yet the darkness does not receive it. We naturally do not receive the light of nature, and yet that light shines, so that we are without excuse. But then also, in this majestic sentence in John **1:5**, there is an element of salvific revelation (it isn't just about the light of nature or creation). So Romans 3:21 tells us that "the righteousness of God has been made known"; God has revealed himself as the way of salvation in Christ, that saving light is shining at the **incarnation** and at the crucifixion and resurrection; and that light is also present here in this verse in John 1. As Carson puts it:

> "The 'darkness' in John is not only absence of light, but positive evil (3:19; 8:12; 12:35, 46; 1 John 1:5-6; 2:8-9, 11); the light is not only revelation bound up with creation, but with salvation … it is quite possible that John … wants his readers to see in the Word both the light of creation and the light of the **redemption** the Word brings in his incarnation." (*John*, pages 119-120)

The Son of God and the Children of God

In John **1:6-9** we meet John, the man often known as John the Baptist. Here in John's Gospel he is described as John the Witness (**v 7-8**). John is introduced here, and then we will hear more about him in the rest of chapter 1 from **verse 19** onwards.

John the Witness's preaching was so powerful that some might have been liable to think that he himself was the Word. The author John was careful to make sure that no one could misunderstand: John was only a witness to the Word (**v 8**), which John (the author) also calls "the light" (**v 4-5, 8-9**), employing another technique of his—different **metaphors** pointing to the same reality.

From **verses 10 to 14a**, John again describes the Word. This time, he describes the response of people to the Word when he became flesh. He came to "his own"—that is, Israel—and they did not receive him or recognize him (**v 11**). He came to "the world" he had made, all peoples, and they did not recognize him either (**v 10**). "Yet to all who did receive him … he gave the right to become children of God" (**v 12**). The early **church father** Chrysostom commented:

> "He became Son of man, who was God's own Son, in order that he might make the sons of men to be children of God." (*Ancient Christian Commentary on Scripture, New Testament IV*, page 40)

These children are, John (the writer) continues, "born not of natural descent, nor of human decision or a husband's will" (**v 13**); he does not specify exactly how this "new birth" happens, but he does say who did it. When you receive Jesus, now as then, you are "born of God" and become a "child of God." The new birth is of inestimable value. I love the words of the great Victorian preacher C.H. Spurgeon:

> "One grain of faith [in Christ] is worth more than a diamond the size of the world—yes, though you should thread such jewels together, as many as the stars of heaven for number, they would be worth nothing compared with the smallest atom of faith in Jesus Christ, the eternal Son of God."
> (*Sermon #2259*, Volume 38)

This is the work of God himself. Jesus will explain more about this new birth later in John 3 when he is quizzed by Nicodemus.

Then in **1:14b-18**, we return to "the witness." If the first verse of the Gospel was profound because it described the **pre-existent**, personal, eternal *logos* as fully God, these verses are even more profound because they describe this *logos* as also fully human flesh. The Reformer John Calvin outlines something of what this signifies:

> "Christ, when he became man, did not cease to be what he formerly was, and that no change took place in that eternal essence of God which was clothed with flesh. In short, the Son of God began to be man in such a manner that he still continues to be that eternal Word who had no beginning of time."
> (*Calvin's New Testament Commentaries*, Vol. 1, pages 20-21)

The Bible claims that Jesus was fully God and fully man in one Person. John puts it like this: "We have seen his glory, the glory of the one and only Son, who came from the Father, full of grace and truth" (**v 14b**). The Word "dwelt" or "tabernacled" among us. God, in the Old Testament, commanded that a tabernacle be put up in the desert as the place where he symbolically dwelt (Exodus 40:34). Then, when King Solomon finally built God's glorious temple in Jerusalem, the glory of God filled that place (2 Chronicles 7:1-3). But now the real and full glory of God dwelled with—"tabernacled"—with people in the very person of Jesus the Christ. Through his Spirit he tabernacles with us still today:

> "There is a place where God does still meet with man and hold fellowship with him. That place is the Person of the Lord Jesus Christ, 'in whom dwells all the fullness of the Godhead bodily.' The manhood of Christ is become to us the **anti-type** of that tent in the center of the camp! God is in Christ Jesus! Christ Jesus is God! And in his blessed Person, God dwells in the midst of us as in a tent." (Spurgeon, *Sermon #1862*, Volume 31)

In John **1:15**, we hear the summary of John the Witness's message: "He who comes after me has surpassed me because he was before me." John is not just saying that Jesus came "before" him because he was the pre-existent, personal, eternal *logos* now in flesh; he is saying that he is "first" of him. He is not just greater, he is the greatest. He is not just before; he is primary, number one, first. Other prophets came before John; Jesus was first: "In the beginning was the Word" (**v 1**) and then "the Word became flesh" (**v 14**).

Jesus is not just greater, he is the greatest.

The next verses not only give a sense of the overflowing blessing and grace that come from receiving Jesus ("one gracious blessing after another"—**v 16**, NLT). They also tell us how the whole Bible, Old Testament and New Testament, fits together:

"Studious attention to the law will reveal the one in whom the grace and truth of God are embodied. The **Torah** itself is a witness to Jesus."

(Hamid-Khani, *Revelation and Concealment of Christ,* page 238)

Jesus, the Word, is preached by all the words of the Bible. Every grace comes from him. This is "grace upon grace" (**v 16**, ESV); the grace of the Law of Moses—which was a response to God's rescue of his people from Egypt—and now the "grace and truth" that "came through Jesus Christ" (**v 17**).

The word "truth" is another key word in John's Gospel. If we have read John's Gospel before, as soon as we hear it, we can think of Jesus saying, "I am the way and the truth and the life. No one comes to the Father except through me" (14:6). We might also think of **Pilate** saying, "What is truth?" (18:38). The truth that came through Jesus Christ is the truth of how to come to the Father. Jesus is the truth, for Jesus is the way to the Father God. If you have seen him, you have seen God. If the "god" we worship is different from Jesus, then that "god" is not the true God. Through Jesus come both grace and truth (**1:17**).

John now concludes his introduction: "No one has ever seen God, but the one and only Son, who is himself God and is in closest relationship with the Father, has made him known" (**v 18**). Essentially, this verse functions as a summary of what John has already written about the Word ("In the beginning was the Word," **v 1**; "the Word became flesh," **v 14**), and about the witness ("We have seen his glory," **v 14**). The rest of the Gospel will now record the witness to this Word.

This revelation of the Son, recorded for us here, calls us to faith, and through personal trust in him, to discovering life and fullness of life in his name. The Gospel of John, each step of the way, will call us to find real life and true life through the real and true Word made flesh.

Questions for reflection

1. If no one has ever seen God, and if God has made himself known in Jesus, how should we answer the person who says, "I would believe in God if I could see him"?

2. Do you struggle more to appreciate the all-powerful divinity of God's Son, or the humble humanity of God's Son? How have these verses helped you?

3. Which single verse from this section could you memorize and call to mind throughout each day to remind you of who God is and who you are?

PART TWO

Not Me, But Him

Humility is a virtue more honored in the breach, and it is more often true than we would like to admit that all our motives are shockingly mixed—all of which makes John the Baptist's approach to Jesus remarkable. So focused was he on who Christ is that he was able to point others to Christ, making sure that his very own followers understood that the really important person was not himself but Jesus. He took, as it were, his huge account of Twitter followers and pointed them to follow another person instead. John is saying, "not me, but him."

> "It is the mark of a truly great man that he can gently, but firmly, detach his followers, so that they may go after a greater."
>
> (Köstenberger, *John*, page 73)

In 1:1-18, we saw how the Word has become flesh that we might believe in him and receive him, and so become children of God, and receive grace upon grace from his fullness. To receive all this from God through faith in Christ means we must actually trust Christ personally, putting our faith in him directly and throughout our lives. Part of grasping that truth of Christ and trusting him is encountering the witnesses that point to Christ. Pre-eminent among them is John the Baptist.

So John, the author of the Gospel, now introduces us to the other John, known as John the Baptist, by means of two stories. Each of them is meant to tell us that John the Baptist was basically a witness. The first story, from **verses 19-28**, tells us that a significant part of John's preaching was telling people that he was nothing special. He was not the Messiah; he was not Elijah returned; nor was he the Prophet (**v 20-21**). He was simply a "voice of one calling in the wilderness" (**v 23**). This first section is John saying, *Not me...* The second story, from **verses 29-34**, which occurs on the "next day" is John saying, *...but him*. These verses then can be summarized by the phrase, *Not me, but him*.

Making the Way Straight

There are, though, many different aspects of these two stories that underline this overall theme of John witnessing to Jesus.

The first, in the first section from **verses 19-28**, is that of **irony**. We are introduced to a group of priests and Levites who have been sent down from Jerusalem by the "Jewish leaders in Jerusalem" (**v 19**). Given that Jerusalem, as a predominantly Jewish city, had many Jews in it, John's way of describing this sending group is a little unusual. What he seems to be indicating is that the elite group who were running things in Jerusalem had got wind of a religious disturbance taking place in the desert region, and were wanting to find out what was going on. So they sent their representatives to John to perform a spot inspection, a bit like a bishop sending his representative to a wayward preacher to discover whether what he is preaching is truly sound. They were performing a "visitation," and they would report what they discovered back to the Jerusalem religious elite (**v 22**). There were Pharisees among them as well (**v 24**)—that strict sect of Judaism that especially emphasized the law. This appears to be a pincer movement upon John's credibility as a preacher: the temple elite (priests and Levites) and the scholarly legal Scripture elite (the Pharisees) are both descending upon John and are about to quiz him as to his soundness. We know from the other Gospels (Matthew 3; Mark 1:1-11; Luke 3:1-22) that John was a rather alarming figure. He would have been quite young too. He wore strange clothes, lived in strange places, and apparently—so they heard—had a strange message (Mark 1:4-8).

As Carson points out, in his appearance and in his message:

"John resembled the Old Testament prophets who sought to call out a holy remnant from the descendants of **Abraham**, and anticipated Jesus' insistence that his messianic community would transcend the barriers of race and depend on personal faith and new birth (Matthew 8:5-12; John 3:1-16)." (*John*, page 146)

It was important that they got to the bottom of things and brought the matter to a head so that John could either be corrected or (if he proved resistant) marginalized and brought down, undermining his influence.

The irony of this event, which must have felt distinctly alarming to John as he preached away in the desert, is brought out by John the author with a subtle twist of words. These representatives had been "sent" by the Jerusalem elite to John (John **1:19**), but John himself had been "sent" by God (v 6)! Who was going to win that encounter? The elite were sending their representatives to test out whether God's representative was **kosher**!

In **verse 23**, John the Baptist very carefully answers by quoting from the Bible (Isaiah 40:3). He uses the words of one of the greatest Old Testament prophets to explain that his role is to "make straight the way for the Lord." John is saying that his message is the same as the message of the Old Testament. The Old Testament was designed to point people to God's Son, his Redeemer, his Messiah, the Christ, Jesus, the Word made flesh. That was the whole purpose—at a macro, big-picture level—of the Old Testament. John is saying that he is not the fulfillment of that Old Testament, but instead is preaching the same message as the Old Testament. This is why it is helpful to think of John as the greatest of the Old Testament preachers. They pointed to Jesus from a distance; John alone saw Jesus and pointed directly to him. But their message was all the same: *Not me, but him.*

John, of course, is baptizing (John **1:25**), and this raises questions, just as it still does today. No one really knows where the Jewish practice of ritual washing and baptizing came from originally. It seems that the fact that John was baptizing did not need explaining (and therefore John was using an already-existing practice), but *why* he was baptizing did require explanation. Archaeologists have discovered baths for ritual washings, and it appears that John was fitting into an already-existing pattern of "baptism of repentance" (Mark 1:4). Centuries before, Naaman the Syrian had been immersed in the water of the Jordan on the instructions of the prophet Elisha (2 Kings 5). What is more, Israel as a whole country had come through the "waters of baptism" when they went through the Red Sea safely and were rescued from the Egyptian army (Exodus 14; see 1 Corinthians 10:2). By offering baptism, John is saying that a great new stage of redemption is about to occur, and he is inviting those who are willing to receive this "Word" to come to the waters of baptism in order to be ready. John makes this point clear when he says, "I baptize with water ... but among you stands one you do not know. He is the one who comes after me, the straps of whose sandals I am not worthy to untie" (John **1:26-27**). In other words, *Not me*. All this took place in Bethany (**v 28**).

Look, the Lamb of God!

But who is this other person, who as yet they "do not know" (introduced in **verse 26**)? The "next day" John will show them (**v 29**). Jesus comes to them, and John recognizes him and tells them that "this is the one" (**v 30**): *Not me, but him*. "Look, the Lamb of God, who takes away the sin of the world!" (**v 29**).

The point that John the Baptist is making is one that he was particularly capable of preaching because he was the son of Zechariah, a priest. He knew about the sacrifice of lambs. He would have seen them sacrificed at the temple at Passover. John is saying that all that—all that memory of the Passover event, when Israel remembered how God had rescued them from Egypt and had passed over them when executing his judgment—was now fulfilled. In Egypt, God had sent his judgment on everyone, and all people, Israelite and Egyptian alike, were liable to that terrible judgment. But those who were covered by the sacrificial lamb—by the blood of that lamb daubed on the door posts—were passed over. There was a sacrifice in their place.

Any thinking person would have asked themselves whether a lamb was really a sufficient sacrifice for a person, let alone whether it really satisfied the righteous requirements of the law and of a blazingly holy God. *Now*, John is saying, *it is all explained*. Here he is: that (the Passover) was about this (Jesus). He is "the Lamb of God, who takes away the sin of the world" (**v 29**).

Really, the whole Exodus story is being fulfilled in reverse. Those who are repentant are being baptized, and the Passover Lamb walks among them. He is far more than John, his ultimate origin demonstrating his infinite superiority (**v 30**; see v 15, **27**). Indeed, John did not at first know him, but the baptism ministry of John had its goal and intention in revealing Jesus for who he really is (**v 31**). This revelation of Jesus takes place in a supernatural event confirming his identity (**v 32**).

John's witness to Jesus is confirmed by a specific divine instruction he had been given that the Spirit of God would descend from heaven on the Messiah, and that this would be how John would recognize him (**v 33**). It is important to understand what John (the author) is saying and what he is not saying. John is not saying that at this moment Jesus became fully God. How could John be saying that when a few verses before he had told us that this Word was God (v 1), full of grace and truth (v 14), the only God, **begotten**, not made, and of one being with the Father, as the creeds put it?

What John (the author) is saying is that Jesus is the Spirit-anointed Author of life. Creation hovers behind this terminology. Genesis 1:2 tells us that "the Spirit of God was hovering over the waters." This Word who created all, and is the Creator, is now baptized in these waters, and the Spirit of God once more "hovers" over them. God the Father, Son, and Holy Spirit rejoice together at this moment when their rescue plan for the world, the Word of God made flesh, is recognized by John the Baptist. The symbol of a "dove" (John **1:32**) specifically resonates with another Old Testament image, and offers peace and the calming of the waters of God's wrath: the dove of Noah, which was sent out after the flood had subsided to show that God's wrath was satisfied and peace had returned (Genesis 8:8-12). Reading this part of John 1 in light of Genesis makes it clear who Jesus is—"God's Chosen One" (John **1:34**)—and John is an eye-witness of this fact. He has "seen" and has "testified" to Jesus. The Word of God incarnate is seen; and the one who sees him, now recognizes him, and having recognized him, he faithfully bears witness.

We too, who through his written word encounter the incarnate Word—we who have heard and recognized—are to follow John the Baptist's example of not only "seeing" but also "testifying." How could we structure the pattern of our daily lives around making a priority of giving witness to what we know about Jesus?

One of the most surprising evangelistic sermons ever preached came from the heart of this passage: "Look, the Lamb of God, who takes away the sin of the world!" (**v 29**). C.H. Spurgeon was practicing with the acoustics in a massive auditorium before he spoke there, and was testing those acoustics by means of saying this resounding text. A janitor, the story goes, heard the sentence "Look, the Lamb of God, who takes away the sin of the world!" and was converted on the spot. It is as we look at that Lamb, rather than at ourselves, our problems, or other people, and it is as we call others away from centering on themselves to centering on him, that we find, and offer, life. Life in all its fullness—that great sub-theme of John—percolates through our beings as we behold, not ourselves, but him—the Lamb who takes away our sins.

Questions for reflection

1. "Not me, but him." To what extent does this attitude characterize your life? How could it do so more (be specific)?

2. Answer the question posed in the penultimate paragraph: How could *you* structure the pattern of your daily life around making a priority of giving witness to what you know about Jesus?

3. "Look, the Lamb of God, who takes away the sin of the world!" In less than a minute, how could you use that verse to explain to a non-Christian what Jesus offers them?

2. A TALE OF TWO CITIES AND A WEDDING

Charles Dickens' famous book *A Tale of Two Cities* begins with an equally famous line:

"It was the best of times, it was the worst of times…"

The story in front of us is structured around a similar plot device—a tale of two cities. And likewise, it has a rhetoric that draws the reader into the story: "Come and see" (**v 39, v 46**). Let the call of this passage to "come and see" draw you in to spend time watching, learning, and seeing Christ in fresh and new ways, and so be encouraged, uplifted, and set upon a new path of following Jesus. You may also find this passage challenges you to leave behind other "focal points" and follow Jesus more completely and thoroughly in your heart and in your life.

The first "city" is Bethsaida (**v 44**). Philip is from Bethsaida, as are Andrew and Peter (**v 44**; Nathanael is from Cana in Galilee—see 21:2). The other disciple who is unnamed in this story (**1:37**) is also presumably from the same town as his companion Andrew. It is there, "the next day" (**v 35**), that John the Baptist points out Jesus again as "the Lamb of God," who takes away the sin of the world (**v 36**). Two men follow Jesus (**v 37**). They want to know where he is staying (**v 38**), so that they can know Jesus better and watch how he is living (an integral part of following a rabbi and of mentorship then as well as now). "Seeing" is a key word in John, as Köstenberger explains:

"'Seeing,' together with 'finding' and 'knowing,' [is] part and parcel of the Johannine witness **motif** [and] relates to witnessing the revelation of God offered by Jesus. The invitation to 'come and see' (also used by other rabbis in Jesus' day) also implies an offer to go and find out together." (*John*, page 82)

Jesus invites them by saying, "Come … and you will see" (**v 39**). Andrew plays a part that is so often under-emphasized, even under-appreciated, but is so often central to the progress of the gospel. "The first thing Andrew did was to find his brother Simon … And he brought him to Jesus" (**v 41-42**). Andrew is less known to posterity than Simon (or, as he is usually called, "Peter"), but without Andrew's ministry of "bringing" there would have not been Peter's ministry of "preaching." Is it due to the downplaying of the role of personal evangelism—of individual, faithful, unheralded witnessing—that our churches are so weak? Is it because we do not emphasize one-on-one discipleship conversations over a cup of coffee that we do not see more great leaders and preachers? If we do not have Andrews, then, under God's **providence**, we are unlikely to have Peters.

If you are a "Peter" you will know who the "Andrews" were in your life. Perhaps take a moment to thank them and encourage them now. If you are an "Andrew," let this section of this passage encourage you that the fruit of your personal ministry is profound, pervasive, and influential. Keep on being an Andrew.

Fishtown and the House of God

This all takes place on "the next day" (**v 35**), but then "the next day" after (**v 43**), Jesus leaves for Galilee. He finds Philip, and he calls him (**v 43**). Philip finds Nathanael and tells him that this is the one that Moses spoke about (**v 45**). Nathanael has an objection—Jesus apparently comes from Nazareth (**v 46**)! Nazareth was a town that probably gave its occupants the peculiarity of speaking with a culturally different, probably less sophisticated accent (Matthew 26:73); and it also was not listed as the "city of **David**," the promised birthplace of the Messiah (Micah 5:2-4). Nathanael does not know what readers of Matthew or Luke today do—that Bethlehem was indeed the birthplace of the man he is being asked to come and meet (Luke 2:4-7, 11).

Then things get strange. Jesus tells Nathanael that he (Nathanael) "truly is an Israelite" (John **1:47**), and when Nathanael asks Jesus how he knows him (thereby accepting Jesus' designation of him as a true Israelite), Jesus says he saw him "under the fig tree" (**v 48**). There has been unending speculation as to what Jesus intended by this, but it certainly has a specific, dramatic impact upon Nathanael, who responds with, "You are the Son of God" (**v 49**). Then Jesus says to Nathanael, "You will see greater things than that" (**v 50**)—essentially, *You ain't seen nothing yet*—and we move on to the famous scene of the wedding in Cana of Galilee.

What on earth is this all about?!

Remember those two cities? That's the key. John is telling the story to contrast "Bethsaida" (meaning literally "fishtown") with indications of another city which would have been famous, and was referenced by Jesus' specific words that on him "the angels of God [are] ascending and descending" (**v 51**). This sounds really weird, sentimental, and obscure. But actually it is echoing another city. You would have to have not only familiarity with the Old Testament but a sensitivity to messianic overtones to pick up the reference. Nathanael understood it immediately. Jesus was referencing the most famous Old Testament narrative of the one who was (in some ways) the original Israelite: Jacob. Later he was renamed "Israel" (Genesis 35:10); and so Nathanael is being called a true Israelite in the sense that he is truly in that line of God's promise for Israel, or Jacob.

Jacob's most famous encounter with God takes place in Genesis 28, where he had a dream in which he saw a stairway, and on it "the angels of God were ascending and descending" (28:12). Sound familiar? And the name of that place, designated by Jacob himself, was Bethel. Bethel means "house of God."

It's a tale of two cities: Bethsaida, fishtown, versus Bethel, God town. And the center of "God town" is Jesus himself, who is the true "stairway to heaven," the true Jacob's ladder. The "greater things" that Nathanael will see (John **1:50**) are Jesus' death, resurrection, and **ascension**, as Jesus himself provides the means of access to God. Jesus is the true "Bethel," the true house of God, and the city of God all centers upon him.

Faith Under the Fig Tree

There is, however, one other aspect of this "tale of two cities" that remains unexplained. What was Nathanael doing "under the fig tree" (**v 48**)? Doubtless Jesus' ability to see him there is another example of Jesus' supernatural power—of a divine nature that Nathanael recognizes even now. Many different possibilities, some more fanciful than others, have been mooted as to what Nathanael was up to. Praying? A secret sin? Apparently it was something more significant than taking a nap.

The idea that Jesus saw something sinful, about which Nathanael was now convicted, is reasonably popular, but the trouble with that view is that whatever Nathanael was doing, it showed Jesus that Nathaniel was "an Israelite in whom there is no deceit" (**v 47**). It's hard to believe that Nathanael doing something deceitful would show Jesus he was someone who was not deceitful.

One approach is to step back from the question of what Nathanael was doing to ask instead why it was so significant. That's an easier question to answer, and it may shed light on what Nathanael was doing, even if it cannot reveal it totally. The fig tree, in Hebrew thinking, was associated with Israel, and in particular with prosperity, in the sense of flourishing under God's favor. It was part of the blessing of the **promised land** (Deuteronomy 8:8); part of the good blessing of that land as opposed to illegitimate rule (Judges 9:10-11, 14); a sign of God's blessing (1 Kings 4:25), to which invaders appealed to try to win over the unwary (2 Kings 18:31); a sign of God's discipline when removed (Jeremiah 8:13); and part of the promised messianic blessing (Micah 4:4), specifically described as sitting "under" a fig tree (Zechariah 3:10).

So, a fig tree was associated with Israel; Jacob's famous dream "ascending and descending" is referenced; Nathanael is a true Israelite; and he is sitting specifically "under the fig tree." It's not quite like saying that Nathanael was "saluting the flag," but it's close. Whatever Nathanael was doing, it was an expression of his commitment to God, and in particular to God's promise that Nathanael now realizes is to be fulfilled in Christ specifically.

In the midst of all this narrative of two cities—and the call of Nathanael to Bethel, to Jesus, the center of God's purposes in the city of God, Jacob's ladder through whom heaven is opened—there is, as we have seen, the unsung roles of Andrew and Philip. Andrew went out and found Peter (which means "the rock," and was an affectionate nickname used by Jesus in Matthew 16:18—here in John's Gospel no further interpretation is given as to its meaning), and Philip found Nathanael (John **1:41, 45**). Now, as then, the work of Christ is progressed through the personal witness, ministry, and invitation of individual disciples. Calvin wrote:

> "We must not be afraid that Christ will hold back from us or deny us early access, if only He sees us striving towards Him. No, indeed! He will stretch out His hand to help our exertions. And will He not hasten to those who come to Him, He who seeks afar off the wandering and astray, to bring them back into the right road?" (*Calvin's New Testament Commentaries*, Vol. 1, page 36)

Are we asking people to focus primarily on us, or on Christ?

Here, then, we are called to "come and see" by means of this comparison between the two cities and the examples of Andrew and Nathanael, Simon and Philip. Let us check where we are calling people to focus: are we asking people to focus primarily on us or on our "ministries," or primarily on the person of Christ himself? It is too easy to begin to "market," or even "sell" our religion, rather than to call people to behold the Lamb of God. The difference is subtle, for we must be active in calling people to follow Jesus, and this surely does require proclamation, promotion, and active public persuasion that Christ is the Lamb of God, who takes away the sin of the world. But though the difference is subtle, it is crucial; in our hearts, we must set apart Christ as Lord, seek to bring people to love him rather than love us, and let the savor of that commitment spread out as a sweet aroma to all those whom we serve for Christ's sake.

But let us also check where we are spending our time. It is striking that the disciples, when they saw where Jesus was staying, "spent that day with him" (**v 39**). Where do we spend our time? How do we use the precious hours of leisure time that are allotted to us? In entertainment, or in the house of the Lamb of God? It is in being "with him" that we will find true rest, renewal, energy, love, grace, and the sheer joy that comes from beholding him. With unveiled faces we behold him, being changed from one degree of glory to another (2 Corinthians 3:18, ESV). Spend time today simply beholding him. Look at him, not to practice a mechanistic technique or learn an intellectual lesson, but to enjoy and love him. In relationship with him, by his Spirit, spend a day with him, and worship him.

And, as you do, expect glorious things: heaven open, the angels of God ascending and descending on the Son of Man. As you focus on him, you will focus on the cross, the great hope for the world, the connection between God and mankind, and the entrance way to glory. That miraculous person, Christ, is glorious—and in the next chapter, we'll watch him beginning to reveal that glory in one of his most famous miracles.

Questions for reflection

1. Who were, or are, the "Andrews" in your life? How will you thank them today for bringing you to come and see Jesus?

   — Roomate in college

2. To whom could you be an Andrew? Who, this week, will you invite to "come and see" Jesus, and how will you do this?

3. Are you beholding Jesus, and how? And do you do so in expectation of seeing glorious things? Do you need to pray that you would see his glory as you read on through John's Gospel?

PART TWO

Wine, Woman, and Song

Who would have thought it? Jesus shows his glory, the very first of the seven signs of John's Gospel (**2:11**), at a wedding (**v 1-2**)—a massive, long party. And not only does he do it at a party, but he does it by producing gallons of wine (**v 6-9**)—so much wine that it would have been impossible to have drunk it all at the party. Whoever this Jesus is, he is not what religion has made him out to be. He is about fullness, and so, in Spurgeon's inimitable words:

"When you are told to believe in him, believe in him up to the brim! When you are told to love him, love him up to the brim! When you are commanded to serve him, serve him up to the brim!" (*Sermon #2317,* Volume 38)

Jesus' glory is shown in this moment of joy (**v 11**). God's new work in Jesus is going to be centered on celebration, joy, festival, and that sign of the **new covenant**, wine.

Verse 4 has often troubled people. Why does Jesus apparently address his mother so bluntly as "woman"? It is important to compare this with 19:26, where Jesus uses the same expression, "woman," when ensuring that his mother will be looked after when he has died. There it is clearly meant in a tender, kind, compassionate sense of a son making sure that his mother is protected when he cannot protect her. In this passage too, then, we may read it as having a similar meaning. In our culture, we do not address a woman as "woman" without disrespect. But the way it was used then in that culture and in that language was as a polite and courteous expression, perhaps more like "Lady" in English, or "Madame" in French. It was not a sentimental expression, but nor was it rude.

The "hour" that has not yet come (**2:4**) is, of course, Jesus' coming hour of death and resurrection. Jesus does not want to be prematurely driven toward the cross by creating too much disturbance before it is the right time, and before he has trained his disciples and completed his teaching.

Jesus' mother says, "Do whatever he tells you" (**v 5**), submitting to Jesus' leadership, and Jesus comes up with a solution that both solves the problem (**v 3**) of this bad party, and also is the first of his seven signs—a sign that shows his glory (**v 11**).

The Pulpit of a Marriage

What is it about this sign that reveals Jesus' glory?

First, it takes place at a wedding. Throughout the Old Testament, weddings and marriage had been symbolic of God's relationship with his people. The prophet Hosea especially played off this theme, but its roots are found in Genesis 2. Paul tells us that marriage is a mystery designed by God to show us Christ's love for the church (Ephesians 5:32). Part of what is revealed here, then, is Jesus' special, joyful love for his people at this wedding. Jesus first reveals his glory not at a funeral, not at a business meeting, not at a sport competition, but at a wedding. The significance of this moment is picked up by the Anglican Book of Common Prayer, which begins each wedding service with these words:

"Holy Matrimony ... is an honorable estate, instituted of God in the time of man's innocency, signifying unto us the mystical union that is betwixt Christ and his Church; which holy estate Christ adorned and beautified with his presence, and first miracle that he wrought, in Cana of Galilee."

It is important to realize that here Jesus confirms the significance, and high calling, of marriage:

"It is traditional to invoke Jesus' presence at the wedding as setting the seal of his approval on the divine ordinance of marriage—and rightly so." (F. F. Bruce, *The Gospel of John*, page 68)

If we are married, we are to see our marriages not only as places in which we encourage each other, and as vehicles for bringing up

> Our marriages are platforms and pulpits for revealing the Christ.

any children we might have, but also as pedestals, platforms, pulpits for revealing the Christ, who adorned this marriage in Cana, and of whom all Christian marriages are intended to speak. Make it your practice to pray together, read the Bible together, and speak of Christ to each other and to others. How we each live out our marriage commitment is one of the most powerful ways that we have to proclaim Christ's glory.

The fact that Jesus is at a wedding may also pick up on the Jacob motif of the previous passage. There, Jesus describes himself as the true Jacob: "'the angels of God ascending and descending on' the Son of Man" (John **1:51**). At that point in the story of Jacob in Genesis 28, Jacob is embarking on a long search for the right wife. Eventually, though unintentionally, he will end up with two wives, Rachel and Leah, and have to serve out his time for fourteen years for those two wives. Marrying the right wife, and enjoying the right kind of wedding, is in the background to the whole Jacob story. Now, here in John's Gospel, having established himself as the true Jacob in his conversation with Nathanael, the next event ("On the third day," John **2:1**) is a wedding. Jesus becomes the sommelier at this wedding by providing gallons of the best wine for the guests. He is redeeming the mistaken weddings of the past by fulfilling the divine intention of all weddings, with his love for God's people.

The Blushing Water

But, of course, this is not just a wedding. This is a wedding at which a guest does something quite extraordinary.

The second aspect of this passage that reveals Jesus' glory, then, is the sheer miracle itself. Turning water into wine is not something that normal people can do. A famous line often attributed to the eighteenth-century English poet Alexander Pope summarizes it best: "The conscious water saw its Master and blushed" (though as far as I can tell, it was first penned—in a slightly different form—by the seventeenth-century poet Richard Cranshaw). The sheer power, **sovereignty**, might, and lordship of Jesus are shown by his turning water into wine. He does not need time; he does not need extra ingredients; he does not perform some magic ceremony. He simply instructs the servants to do as he asks (**v 7-8**), and there is wine instead of water.

Some may wonder how this is possible. How can water become wine? Naturally, it cannot (at least, not in this instant way). John is not making a claim to Jesus having discovered some hidden property of H_2O. The point is that Jesus is the Creator and the Sustainer of all things. To move molecules and atoms and change the basic biochemical reality of a substance is not difficult for him. It takes no effort; he does not work up a sweat; it is not demanding. "The conscious water saw its Master and blushed."

Of course, Christians do not believe that miracles happen all the time—otherwise they would not be miracles. Even in John's Gospel, they are comparatively rare; in the Bible as a whole they are rarer, and in the experience of most people they are extremely rare. That is what makes them miracles! But because of who God is, it is not philosophically nor scientifically problematic to accept that miracles are possible. If Jesus is that Creator God, then we should expect miracles to be performed by him.

In this view of things, the normal course of events—the standard laws of physics—are an expression of God's constant character and are the norm that we can expect as we do work in history, or science, or medicine, or banking. When we apply the brakes on our cars or examine substances under a microscope, we expect them to behave according to the laws of physics. But where do those laws come from? What allows us to be so confident that they are constants upon which we may rely? Jesus here steps in to do something different to indicate that he is the One who makes water (and wine) as it normally is according to the standard operation of nature. Like Alfred Hitchcock appearing in one of his movies, so Jesus writes himself into the story, and does something that only the author of the story could do. Then we are able to see his glory: that is, to see him for who he really is. F.F. Bruce points out that:

> "Jesus' action was, in C.S. Lewis's terminology, a 'miracle of the old creation': the Creator who, year by year, turns water into wine, so to speak, by a natural process, on this occasion speeds up the process and attains the same end."

> (*The Gospel of John*, page 72)

To worship Jesus means to worship the one who here revealed his glory—"the glory of the one and only Son ... full of grace and truth" (1:14). Oftentimes we constrain Jesus to operating within the parameters of what we can explain, and we live lives of timidity because we think of him as only capable of certain kinds of interventions or actions, all within the normal course of events. It is not right, nor rational, to expect miracles at every moment, since they thereby stop being miracles at all—but that said, we do worship the Jesus who is God himself, and more than capable of intervening on our behalf. He hears and answers prayers. We cannot escape from his presence, nor outlive the extent of his power. Risking our lives for God—through missionary commitment, through standing up for morality and truth, through holding fast to living holy lives even when the commitment is difficult—makes sense when we realize that the Jesus we follow is *this* Jesus.

Wine Instead of Washing

The third aspect of this sign that reveals Jesus' glory is seen in a comparison with the practice of Judaism at the time. The "six stone water jars" (**2:6**) are for the Jewish rites of purification. They are very large containers, each holding twenty or thirty gallons. These purification jars—vessels for ritual washing of a religious kind—are taken over by Jesus to be used as dispensers of wine for a party! How much more clearly could Jesus make his point?! A new day is here, and it is a day of joy, of celebration, of partying, of feasting, of a wedding! Wine is a standard image in the Old Testament of the new-covenant blessing to come (e.g. Joel 3:18). Whereas in the ritual washing of the day there were all sorts of special occasions requiring special washing, now, under Jesus' lordship, all that is turned to wine!

> "Christ has come into the world to fulfill and terminate the old order, and to replace it by a new worship … which surpasses the old as much as wine surpasses water."
>
> (Bruce, *The Gospel of John,* page 72)

The fourth part of this sign that reveals Jesus' glory is the wine itself. This is not any old cheap wine, but the very best (John **1:10**). It is instructive of who Jesus is that when he turns water into wine, it is not a poor kind, but the best. It was probably normal practice to bring out the lower-quality wine after the guests had drunk enough not to notice. But when Jesus brings out the wine, even though it is last, it is an excellent, high-quality vintage. In so doing Jesus reveals his "glory" (**v 11**), and his disciples "believed in him." When we see Jesus for who he truly is—when we grasp his beauty and glory—then we are moved toward faith in and commitment to him.

The wedding over, Jesus then goes down to Capernaum (**v 12**), and stays with his mother and brothers and disciples. Since Jesus had brothers, apparently his mother had had other children after Jesus was born.

The Hallmark of the Christian

There are certainly many reasons to lament in life—and indeed there are portions of Scripture, including many of the psalms, which help us, when we face sadness and difficulties, to work through our feelings in the context of God's hope and power. But the nature of the gospel in which we believe is that it is good news, and with it comes joy. Joy is the hallmark of the Christian, for every Christian knows the things about which we can be joyful even when all other joys are taken from us. Like Paul and Silas, we can sing in jail—and that glorious truth, that glorious joy, can be the song in our hearts even down the darkest dale and in the deepest pit. The real Jesus is the Jesus who turned water into wine, and who did his first miracle at a party, a wedding. Would you receive his joy again today, by his Spirit—that supernatural joy that only he can give—and let him, as it were, turn your water into wine?

Questions for reflection

1. "Jesus first reveals his glory not at a funeral, not at a business meeting, not at a sport competition, but at a wedding." Would people close to you get that sense of what Jesus is like, by looking at you and your life and speech?

2. How are you most likely to constrain Jesus to the parameters of what you can explain? How does that affect your prayer life?

3. How will knowing the Jesus who turns water to wine give you joy today?

3. JESUS V FAKE RELIGION

For many people today, one of the greatest barriers to true faith in God is fake religion. It is possible to have a significant enough exposure to "religion" that it functions as a sort of inoculation against the real thing. There is a human tendency to turn God's miraculous, supernatural grace-filled message into a mechanistic technique for furthering human pride, power, wealth, or privilege. This has always been a problem, because humans are sinful, and without constant exposure to God's word and the power of God's Spirit we all too easily default to **legalism**, **Pharisaism**, or moral **depravity**—even within the bounds of so-called "religion."

And now along comes this section of John to countermand all of that with God's word. This part of John's Gospel—Jesus driving the money changers out of the temple—is one of the most famous in the Bible, as well as one of the most frequently misinterpreted.

The story itself is again fairly straightforward and familiar, but it is also so remarkable that it is well worth rehearsing. Near the time of the Passover, Jesus goes up to Jerusalem (**v 13**). He makes his way to the temple courts (**v 14**), but there discovers, evidently to his horror, a commercial enterprise in full swing. People are selling cattle and sheep and doves, and others are exchanging money. The temple courts have become a significant place of business transactions. In response, Jesus makes "a whip out of cords" (**v 15**)—not a particularly dangerous or vicious kind of whip—and drives these people who are making money in the temple out of the temple. He even turns over their tables, presumably scattering the coins themselves with a resounding series of clangs onto the stone floor. *Get these out of here!* Jesus cries. *How dare you turn my Father's house into a market!* (**v 16**).

His disciples, of course, wonder what Jesus is doing. Being well-versed in the Bible, they remember an Old Testament text that they think will explain Jesus' apparently intemperate actions: "Zeal for your house will consume me" (**v 17**). The Jewish leaders are less forgiving, and demand an explanation and, in particular, miraculous proof of his authority (**v 18**). Jesus replies with one of his most famous—and shocking—aphorisms: if they destroy this temple, he will raise it again in three days (**v 19**).

The Jewish leaders cannot understand what Jesus could possibly mean by this, and in case we find ourselves as readers in the same situation, John explains for us (**v 20-22**). Jesus is speaking of his own resurrection from the dead, teaching us that the temple is fulfilled in himself and his death and resurrection. Since the "temple" was the place where God's people could access the presence of God, the Old Testament temple building was always about pointing to Jesus himself. At the time the disciples did not understand what Jesus was saying, but when Jesus was raised from the dead, they remembered his teaching and believed (**v 21-22**).

Who Do You Trust?

The story concludes with John's comment that, while many believed in Jesus when they saw the miraculous signs he was doing (**v 23**), Jesus would not entrust himself to people, "for he knew all people" (**v 24**); he "knew what was in each person" (**v 25**). Why does Jesus not "entrust himself to them"? The answer is that he "knew what was in each person." Jesus understood that humans are far from perfect, just as anyone does if they read God's word, and inwardly digest the evidence of their eyes and the lessons of history and of their own hearts. We all have a lamentable tendency to do what which is not "trustworthy."

Jesus' example here does not mean that his followers should live in constant wariness, lacking emotional intimacy with friends, let alone spouses. It does mean, though, that our ultimate and total "trust" can only really be in God. Only he, and only his promises, will never let us down. It is only Jesus who is utterly trustworthy and utterly reliable, and at some point or other even those nearest and dearest to us will die before we die, or we will die before they die. Once we have rejected the idolatry of entrusting everything we have to another person in what becomes an act of worship, we are actually freer to trust and love and be loyal to people—to treat our fellow humans better, in a way that is more healthy for us. Entrusting ourselves to God, rather than to other people, means we can love others without putting them on a pedestal or being surprised when we discover that they too (like us) are sinners.

What Jesus Hates

The part of this story that most shocks many is Jesus throwing people out of the temple. Some think it means that Jesus sometimes lost his cool, and conclude therefore that on occasions it is okay for us to be angry (a "throwing the money changers out of the temple" moment). Other people argue that it means that when a church meets on a Sunday morning, it should never do any business—not even selling Christian books or literature ("That's money-changing in the temple, so stop it!"). Then there are those who find it all fairly offensive that Jesus (that is, "gentle Jesus, meek and mild") would do something apparently violent or at least aggressive; it seems less than we should expect from the perfect, suffering Servant. What sort of Jesus is this, who whips people and shoves them out of the door (**v 15**)?

The answer is that this is the kind of Jesus who hates fake religion. He cannot stand it. If there is one thing that makes Jesus livid, it is fake religion, such as he finds here in the temple, as Carson describes:

"Instead of solemn dignity and the murmur of prayer, there is the bellowing of cattle and the bleating of sheep. Instead of brokenness and contrition, holy adoration and prolonged petition, there is noisy commerce." (*John,* page 179)

It is interesting to compare Jesus' response to people caught in fla-grant, immoral sin—those who have done what is clearly wrong—with his reaction to religious leaders who are leading people wrongly, and who think they are doing nothing wrong. He reserves his sharpest opposition for Pharisees, not for prostitutes, and for temple religion gone wrong rather than for people who get drunk at the local pub.

Jesus hates fake religion. And the reason for that is because it blocks access to God.

What was going on with these money changers was not just that they were making money out of people coming to church. They were charging people to change money into temple currency to buy sacri-ficially pure animals for worship. The people who would have been particularly at risk from this extortionate business were those outside the temple religion: God-fearers who were not born as Jews, or those who were not regular in the temple courts. So the point of disgust for Jesus is not the money-making but blocking access to God.

The parallel account in Mark's Gospel makes clear this consequence of the money-changing business: blocking access to God. In Mark 11:17, Jesus quotes from the Old Testament passage that says that God's house should be "a house of prayer for all nations" (Isaiah 56:7). However, the money changers were making money out of peo-ple's desire for God, and in doing so they were making it harder for them to find God. It made Jesus livid.

Hurdles on the Way into Church

The sad truth is that we sometimes do the same today. We make it harder for people to find God, not easier, by turning our "tem-ples" of worship into places that make it tough to have access to God. The point of the temple was to be the place where all people could go to meet with God. The same, in that regard at least, is true for church today. Church, as the Archbishop of Canterbury William Temple once said, is the one institution that exists for the benefit of its non-members. Unfortunately, while that should be true, for many of our churches it is actually not true. Many of our churches structure all of their business, organization and meetings around the preferences of the people who pay the bills. Who has invested in putting up this structure, this building? Who is paying the salary of the staff? Who are the members and what do they want, for after all they have a vote? In other words, we ask "money-changer-like" questions: how can we make sure that what happens here is what will benefit those who are already here? Anyone else who wants to come along will have to jump through certain hoops and get over certain hurdles before we will allow them access to God.

Those hurdles are hard to spot for those who are erecting them. Sometimes it can be cultural matters, such as insider language, that prevent access to God; perhaps we communicate with terminology that no one else could possibly understand. Of course, this does not mean we should lower moral barriers, nor does it mean we should remove doctrinal clarity. It does mean that we should be both culturally and personally welcoming. Our resources as a church should go into making it easier, not harder, for people to hear the gospel, understand the gospel, and respond to the gospel by repenting of their sins and trusting Christ. We are not to prioritize making people comfortable as we preach, for the gospel message cuts sinners sharply; but we do make the gospel "clear," so that the gospel message can hold out its healing and restoration.

John Calvin put it like this:

"The majesty of God which dwells in the Church should always be set before our eyes, that it may not be defiled by any impurities. But its holiness will remain sound only if nothing foreign to the Word of God is admitted to it."

(*Calvin's New Testament Commentaries,* Vol. 1, page 53)

Who Do You Think You Are?

It is important to note that no one is hurt by what Jesus does. His critics in John **2:18** do not charge him with doing damage to property, and certainly not with hurting people (or even animals). If Jesus had damaged someone or something, we can be sure they would have brought that up in their accusation. But, no, their charge is not that Jesus had wounded anyone but that what he had done was display-ing the kind of authority which they did not believe he rightfully pos-sessed. What sort of authority did he have that enabled him to change the operating procedure of the temple? Where did that authority come from? The temple was the place of divine symbolic presence in the world. For someone to come along and clean house there sug-gests a very high level of authority. In essence, they are asking Jesus, *Who on earth do you think you are?!*

Jesus, as he so often does, answers the deeper question behind the question. They ask him, in effect, who he thinks he is (**v 18**), and he replies not simply by asserting his authority, but by asking, in effect, *Well, what do you think the temple is?* (**v 19**): "Destroy this temple, and I will raise it again in three days." The real point he is making is that the religious leaders have misunderstood the role and actuality of the temple. The temple was only ever designed to be a sign of something far greater. They have made the temple the end game, when really it was a sign along the road toward something (and Someone) else.

Of course, they do not understand Jesus' point, and reply by asking how anyone could rebuild this temple in three days, since it has taken forty-six years to build (**v 20**). Here John, in **verse 21**, enters into the narrative with his own interpretation to make sure the reader gets the point that Jesus is making. This temple is not the physical temple that Jesus' critics thought he was talking about. No, the real temple is Jesus. This is not a metaphorical association that Jesus is making. The actual temple is not actually the temple that took forty-six years to build. That's merely a sign of the temple. The real temple *is* Jesus.

What John is explaining, and what Jesus is saying, is that Jesus' death and resurrection are actually the way to find access to God. You do not find access to God through a physical structure, through a temple, through a particular religious place or sanctuary. All that is intended to bring us to Jesus himself. The way to God is through faith in Jesus' death and resurrection.

Christian circles today are not immune from promoting the confusion that Jesus is addressing here. We tend to do it in one of three ways. First, some make the physical church building a temple where access to God is found. Second, others make religious rituals or a certain ceremony, or a particular kind of musical atmosphere, the way to access God. Third (and this is more of a "low church" kind of mistake but still similar in essence), some make the point of access to God a human—a particularly dynamic religious leader, often a Bible teacher with remarkable gifts. At times churches may even emphasize the Bible itself in such a way that "understanding" the Bible becomes a merely intellectual pursuit, and knowledge of the Bible is the ultimate goal, rather than leading people to understand the word of God as the God-given means by which we meet with God himself through his Spirit.

> Our temple is Jesus himself, and Jesus alone.

The temple, though, is not the physical temple. Our temple is Jesus himself, and Jesus alone. So, as Bruce Milne writes:

"Jesus is looking beyond the age of temple worship to the time when worship will be offered in the Holy Spirit on the basis of the sacrificial death of the Lamb of God, who is prefigured in the Passover victims which he had just evicted from the temple. He is claiming nothing less than the reconstituting of the entire worship of God's people around his own person and mission. The temple will pass into oblivion, not only because it is physically razed, but because it is spiritually obsolete. Jesus' body, offered up in sacrifice and raised up in power, will be the new temple where God and humanity, creator and creature, meet face to face." (John, pages 69-70)

Not Yet Time

We discussed the meaning of **verses 24-25** above. Yet their purpose in this narrative appears a little confusing. But they are also part of the growing drama that John is investing into his narrative that connects to the succeeding sections of his book. The time has not yet come. It is not yet Jesus' hour, when he will die and rise again. So in the meantime, Jesus is not going to entrust himself to people who will misinterpret what he is doing and either oppose him, perhaps violently, or try to make him a king or leader, again perhaps violently. People, even his disciples, did not understand what he was saying. It was not yet time for him to be taken to the cross.

But while he would not "entrust himself" to people, the word about Jesus was getting out to people—and some wanted to find out more. As we will see in the next section, one of those with questions about Jesus was even from the elite religious class of Jesus' day.

Questions for reflection

1. What do you think would be the modern-day equivalent of people blocking access to God in church life?

2. What could your church do to make itself welcoming? Are there some "sacred cows" that you need to kill in order to be more inviting?

3. What difference does it make that Jesus, and not a building, is our temple; and that access to God is through him, and not through religious ritual?

PART TWO

Two Rabbis

Few stories resonate more with us today than this one of Nicodemus. This is especially true if you are from a religious or academic background, or part of a leadership group. Nicodemus was all of those— a teacher of significance (**3:10**) and a member of the Jewish ruling council (**v 1**). Even for those of us who have none of these kinds of credentials, the passage nevertheless resonates with us as we see a man who came "at night," hidden, not wanting to be seen, to ask Jesus questions (**v 2**). Many have begun their approach to Jesus under cloak of darkness, not wanting to be called out by their friends as being too interested in the things of God. Not only this, but this passage contains probably the best-known verse in the whole Bible—John **3:16**. But what does it all mean?

Nicodemus comes to Jesus by night and poses an implicit question (**v 2**) that Jesus will spend the remainder of the passage answering. As one of the elite rulers of the Jewish people (**v 1**), conscious no doubt of his own expertize, Nicodemus does not ask Jesus directly. But he implies his request in a statement: "Rabbi, we know that you are a teacher who has come from God. For no one could perform the signs you are doing if God were not with him" (**v 2**). His request is for Jesus to explain to him why Jesus is doing what he is doing. Nicodemus can see that Jesus is performing the signs, but he cannot quite admit that it does not make sense to him. It is possible that he has come to make a "deal" with Jesus, to butter him up with smooth words, in order to encourage him to be less extreme. Or it could be that Nicodemus is a genuine seeker, but too proud to admit that he has many unanswered questions. His approach is a little like someone going to a counselor and saying, "I have a friend who has such-and-such a problem," and it's obvious that the "friend" is little more than a smokescreen for their own problem. So Nicodemus comes along, saying, as one academic rabbi to another, *Let us discuss this question regarding all the signs* *you are a performing.* This was so much code for, *Help me understand why you are doing what you are doing.*

WWJD?

John structures this episode around a single metaphorical theme that indicates that the whole of this section is a developed answer to Nicodemus' implied question (**v 2**). Jesus answers the question in such a way that he ends by referring to "the light" that anyone who genuinely seeks the truth will come into and be happy to be exposed by (**v 19-21**)—the light to which Nicodemus is being exposed as he walks out of the "night."

Imagine the nighttime (**v 2**) when Nicodemus turns up to see Jesus. This is not a dark night as we have in contemporary cities, where there are street lights on all the time. This is an ancient, Middle-Eastern darkness—truly dark, with very few or no man-made lights outside. But there is light where Jesus is.

So Nicodemus, at the dead of night, turns up to see Jesus. He poses a question by making a statement. He couches it (as the proud tend to do) in a statement of what "we know," but of course, if he truly knew the answer already, he would not have come to see Jesus and to find out! The point is that he does not know—or rather, he knows that Jesus is important, but he does not know why he is important.

This darkness in which Nicodemus is enveloped is gradually exposed for what it is, until, by the end of Jesus' answer (**v 21**), the light of Christ is shining on Nicodemus. In all likelihood, Nicodemus ended up, after this encounter, believing in Jesus (7:50; 19:39), or at least he became thereafter susceptible to being persuaded that Jesus was doing something right, even if he did not fully understand or accept at that point exactly who Jesus was. At the end of his conversation with Jesus, he is not there yet: he needs (surprisingly) to be born again:

"There could be few Jews, if any, in the entire city that night whose credentials were more impressive as far as acceptance with God was concerned. Yet, Jesus tells him he needs to be born again." (*Milne,* John, page 75)

Wonderfully, it is quite possible that he received Jesus' challenge to believe.

This passage is answering the question: *WWJD?* Not as that **acronym** is usually explained (What Would Jesus Do?), but instead as *Why* Would Jesus Do this? Nicodemus knows that Jesus is up to something. He knows that he is doing some amazing miracles, some "signs" (**3:2**). But he does not know what the "signs" signify. He does not know why Jesus is doing what he is doing. Why is he performing these signs? Why is this happening? Nicodemus is looking for the right interpretation of Jesus' actions and signs.

Of Water and the Spirit

Jesus' teaching that a person must be "born again" (v 3), born of "water and the Spirit" (**v 5**) to see and enter the kingdom of God seems initially straightforward. Jesus is indicating that it is not enough for someone only to be born naturally; he or she must also be born supernaturally. But the more you think about it, the harder it is to understand exactly why these particular words, "of water and the Spirit," are chosen to make that point.

Some have said that by "water" Jesus means baptism. That, in this context, is unlikely. Of course Jesus is in favor of baptism. He himself was baptized by John the Baptist (Mark 1:9). Jesus had a baptism ministry too (John 3:22), though he did not personally baptize; his disciples did the baptisms (4:2). But in the context of this passage and this conversation with Nicodemus, baptism has not been discussed, and so a mention of "water" by itself does not immediately indicate that Jesus must be talking about baptism.

Many others have suggested that, given the immediate context of human birth to which Nicodemus has just referred (**3:4**), Jesus must be talking about the waters of birth, when a woman's waters break before giving birth, and in this way he is referring to natural birth. While this interpretation fits the context better, some scholars think there is insufficient evidence from other sources that would indicate that "water" was a common way of referring to birth at the time.

A third option is that by "water and the Spirit," Jesus actually means both terms as descriptions of the supernatural birth. There are Old Testament prophetic predictions that refer to the work of the Spirit in the New Testament that link that work to water as well (Ezekiel 36:25-26; Isaiah 44:3). The most likely interpretation, then, seems to be that Jesus is saying in John **3:5** that the Spirit must be poured out like water so that someone is born from above. In which case, both "water" and "the Spirit" refer to the supernatural work of God in causing someone who believes in Jesus to be born again.

Born Again

In **verse 6**, Jesus returns to the same theme, but this time by contrasting what the flesh does (clearly a reference to natural human birth) with what the Spirit does. In order, then, to answer any lingering questions that Nicodemus might have about the possibility of this action (**v 7**), Jesus compares it to wind (**v 8**). This was a well-known comparison, because in Hebrew the word for "wind" and the word for "Spirit" are the same (*ruach*).

However, it becomes clear from Nicodemus' response in **verse 9** that he still does not understand. And, after all, who can blame him? What Jesus is talking about is something entirely different from the normal way of living, and from any other religious program. Jesus is operating in a different zone, proposing a different solution, and talking about a different approach than religion typically does. Nicodemus is scratching his head and wondering how being reborn is feasible.

Jesus gently rebukes Nicodemus (**v 10**). While it is certainly understandable that Nicodemus was flummoxed by Jesus' teaching, Nicodemus really should have known better. He was "Israel's teacher," he was well-versed in the Jewish Scriptures, and what Jesus was talking about was what the Scriptures had promised would happen. If Nicodemus had examined the word more carefully, he would have realized that there was an expectation and a hope for a new work of the Spirit in coordination with this "kingdom of God" that Jesus was bringing. It was not to be a kingdom of might or power, but of the work of the Spirit. Nicodemus does not get that. But, Jesus says, if he had read his Bible more carefully, he really would not have been surprised. Because Jesus is who he is, he speaks of what he knows (**v 11**), but nonetheless his testimony is not received; and if Nicodemus does not believe this teaching, then how will he believe even more heavenly teaching (**v 12**)? Only Jesus, the "Son of Man," is able to speak of such matters, because he is from heaven, but his testimony is not received (**v 13**).

Jesus and the Snake

Jesus next refers to a famous incident—at least, an incident famous for the people of Nicodemus' time: the lifting up of the snake in the wilderness by Moses (**v 14**). God's people were being disobedient, again, complaining against God, and by way of punishment God sent snakes to bite them. In response, God's people repented, and God then told Moses to put a snake on a pole and raise it up; and any of God's people who looked at the snake on the pole lived (Numbers 21:4-9). This was God's way of teaching the Israelites that healing and salvation come through trusting in God and looking at the one he has lifted up. They were healed when they looked (with faith) at the snake on the pole, and therefore were saved.

The point Jesus is making refers to his own "lifting up." As Kösten-berger puts it:

"'Lifted up' has a double meaning here (cf. [John] 8:28, 12:32, 34), linking Jesus' exaltation with his elevation on a cross. The expression draws on Isaiah 52:13." (*John*, page 128)

So Jesus taught later, "When you have lifted up the Son of Man, then you will know that I am he and that I do nothing on my own but speak just what the Father has taught me" (John 8:28). "And I, when I am lifted up from the earth, will draw all people to myself" (12:32). Jesus is teaching Nicodemus about the ultimate source of the power of the Spirit, who is given to those who believe in Jesus: his cross, or in his terms here, his being "lifted up." At the cross, and through faith in Jesus, as we look at him raised up, "everyone who believes may have eternal life in him" (**3:15**).

Light in the Darkness

From here to the end of this section, Jesus explains himself further. The famous **verse 16** fits into this context, which is an explanation of Jesus' sacrifice on the cross as both the superlative expression of God's love for us, and as the means by which it can be possible for anyone who believes in him not to perish but have eternal life. As Calvin put it:

"The true looking of faith, I say, is placing Christ before one's eyes and beholding in him the heart of God poured out in love. Our firm and substantial support is to rest on the death of Christ as its only pledge."

(*Calvin's New Testament Commentaries,* Vol. 1, page 74)

Our condemnation remains if we do not believe in Jesus (**v 18**) because, like the Israelites in the wilderness, we have disobeyed God and complained against his good provision, and we deserve his just condemnation. Justice will mean that we are condemned. In that situation we remain, unless we look at the snake on the pole, unless we look at the one who was condemned for us—the Lord Jesus Christ. If we believe in him, then we are not condemned but instead have eternal life, life now and life forever with Jesus.

> Our better instincts long for the stars but our sins mean we are attracted to the dark.

Now, in **verse 19**, comes the verdict, the conclusion, the summation: "Light [that is, Jesus] has come into the world, but people loved darkness." It is an extraordinary fact, but the **human condition** is such that we all experience a gravitational pull to the black hole of sin's "darkness." Our better instincts may long for the stars, but our evil desires, our sins, mean that we are attracted to "hiding," to being "in the dark," away from the "light," which so uncomfortably reveals our darkness to ourselves, to others, and most scarily of all to God himself. We "will not come into the light for fear that [our] deeds will be exposed" (**v 20**). But when we live "by the truth," then we come "into the light" (**v 21**), so that it may be seen that what is done is done through God.

Sitting there in the darkness is Nicodemus, who has sneaked in to see Jesus late at night, making a statement of what "we know" (we elite, we authoritative rulers, we proud), but actually, implicitly, asking Jesus a question: *Who are you, and why are you doing what you are doing?* As Jesus answers, he shines his "light" into the darkness. The only question is whether Nicodemus, his face shrouded in shadow, will come out into the "light" by believing in the One that God sent to take his punishment for him.

Will we come into the "light"? We will leave "the darkness"? Will we look on him who is "lifted up," the Son of Man, Jesus, and so find salvation through faith in him?

Questions for reflection

1. How would you use these verses to define what it means to be "born again"?

2. How have you been guilty of loving darkness in your own life, or how have you seen that in someone else's? How have you experienced Jesus' light shining into your darkness?

3. How does the image of the snake on the pole make you more grateful for Jesus being "lifted up"?

4. REAPING A STRANGE HARVEST

How can we be more effective and "successful" as Christians, or in Christian ministry and lifestyle? Are there certain techniques that you can learn, particular habits that you can foster, or notable relationships that you need to nurture in order to network your way to the top? Are there special ways in which the church today needs to act in order to have a more effective witness to contemporary culture?

I have just been sent an email link to a story of a church turning its services into a real-ale festival in order to attract more people. Is that kind of "creativity" the answer, or is there another way to be effective witnesses to Jesus in today's society? This is the great question facing the Western church: how do we regain our ability and power to show and share Christ in such a way that other people are drawn to him, notice our witness, and follow Christ too? What is the secret of effective Christian witness, and how do we seize opportunities when they present themselves to us?

No doubt there are many different answers to this question about how to have an effective Christian witness, but this passage reveals an aspect of the right approach regarding witness that is frequently forgotten or under-emphasized.

With the Witness Again

Throughout John's Gospel, the other John (John the Baptist) is described over and over again as a witness. So frequent is this designation of him as the witness that some have said that in John's Gospel he would be better called "John the Witness" rather than "John the Baptist." John is introduced in chapter one as the witness (1:7), and he returns now into the story again as a witness (**3:22-24**). Jesus' disciples are baptizing in the Judean countryside (**v 22**). John is baptizing at Aenon "because there [is] plenty of water" (**v 23**). We are given a historical note to make sure we know where we are in the narrative (**v 24**), and this set-up between Jesus' disciples baptizing and John baptizing where there was plentiful water now leads to a "discussion" between John's disciples and a particular individual about "purification," because baptism would have seemed to some of the Jews to fit into the framework of purification rituals of the time (**v 25**—see 2:6).

Of course, there is something about John's witness that is unique. He saw Jesus (and we do not); he was a prophet in the Old Testament sense (and we are not). He had a particular part to play in God's salvation plan that is different than that of any of us today. And yet John is also a model of witness for us too. He shows what it means to be an effective witness to Christ. There are both challenges and opportunities to effective Christian witness. John surmounts the challenges and makes the most of the opportunities. His model of effective Christian witness is worth noting carefully as well as following confidently.

Jealous Guys

John, the author of the Gospel, presents this story of John the Witness sandwiched between two very well-known stories—that of Nicodemus and that of the woman at the well. Why this story here? It is the last time that John the Witness appears in John's Gospel, but this is more than a fond farewell. It shows us exactly what was so great about John. John, the author of the Gospel, is telling us to witness to Jesus like John the Witness (and not like John's disciples in this story).

John's disciples are jealous. They note that Jesus' disciples are baptizing more people than John (**3:26**). How human is this! And how common for jealousy to be the reason for carefully worded disagreements between people in ministry, and how damaging it is to our witness to Christ. We smuggle under the cloak of witness a dagger of jealousy. We want to be first. We want to be best. We want to be the center of attention. We want to be able to report back to headquarters that our baptism numbers are up. We want to make sure that we are ahead of our rivals for ministry prominence.

In their jealousy, John's disciples were objecting to the core purpose of John's ministry: "Everyone is going to him" (that is, to Jesus), they said (**v 26**). As if they expected John to be disappointed! He had borne witness to Jesus, and now they were all going to Jesus! But somehow they had not internalized the consequences of what John was doing. He had said over and again that he was not "the one," but that someone else was coming who was greater than he, and to whom he was witnessing. Now, however, they were surprised and disappointed when all the people went to the One that John the Witness had pointed them to! How could they be so dim as to object that John had succeeded in witnessing to the One he said he was going to witness to?

What was it that allowed jealousy to flourish to this extent? It is one thing to note the jealousy; it is another thing to explain it. John's answer to their complaint explains both the cause of their mistake and its solution. He understood the challenges and opportunities of effective Christian witness.

The heart of his answer is in **verses 27-28**. Who he is is "given … from heaven … I am not the Messiah but am sent ahead of him." John's point is that this is who he is, as well as who he is not. Effective Christian witness begins with a negative proposition. Much of contemporary Christian witness is ineffective because it forgets this.

Essentially, we are trying to draw people to Jesus by drawing people to ourselves. We make ourselves attractive (or at least we hope to do so) in the vain hope that someone will come to us as we witness to Christ. John's approach is quite different. He confesses freely that he is not the Christ. In essence, his ministry is built around a negative statement. In effect, he is saying, *Oh me? No, I'm nothing special. I don't have any particularly wonderful gifts. I'm not that important. You might not notice it, but I have my hang-ups too. I mess up. I'm not the one that is really interesting. Actually, that's someone else.*

This is very different to much of our witness today. We tend to say, or to sound as though we are saying, *Look at us! Aren't we amazing? Haven't we figured out life? Isn't our intellect so stunning?!* Much contemporary theology goes wrong at this point. You cannot assert the positive side of witness until you have learned the negative. You cannot point people to Christ until you have learned to point them away from yourself. If theologians would learn this lesson, we would have fewer novel ideas presented as the latest, greatest fad, and more headlights on Jesus and his word. We would be less inclined to become defensive or picky because our books were read less than other people's, or our conferences were less well attended. We would begin with a negative.

All calling to ministry must begin with a recognition of this negative. We are the friend of the bridegroom (**v 29**). There is joy in that calling. But it is essentially negative. A friend of the bridegroom is defined by what he or she is not:

"In some real sense the Baptist testified that God himself was in Christ betrothing his bride to himself afresh."

(J. O. F. Murray, *Jesus According to S. John*, page 241)

Creator, Sustainer, and Savior

There is more than a negative here, though—there is also a joyful positive. This is the description of Jesus that begins in **verse 31**. Commentators differ as to whether this properly belongs in the speech of

John the Baptist, or is simply a part of the ongoing narrative of John the author of the Gospel. In some sense it does not really matter. Jesus' speeches are so interwoven with "Johannine style" that you might be forgiven for wondering whether Jesus learned his style from John, rather than the other way around (as was surely the case). Similarly, if John the Witness is speaking from **verse 31**, he is speaking in a way that Jesus sometimes speaks, and also in a way that John the author of the Gospel also writes. Whoever it is who first spoke these words, what matters is that ultimately we are reading God's word, and these verses describe why those who begin with recognizing who they are not are nonetheless filled with joy: Jesus is someone before whom it is a pleasure to play second fiddle (**v 29-30**). He is a faithful witness, even if that witness is not commonly received (**v 32**); and those who do receive it realize that "God is truthful" (**v 33**), for he "speaks the words of God" and "gives the Spirit without limit" (**v 34**)—bountiful blessings indeed.

> Accepting that our purpose is to serve God is not to grovel in the dust but to explore the stars.

"The Father loves the Son and has placed everything in his hands" (**v 35**). This is Jesus: Son of God, the Almighty Lord of all, beloved of the Father. Accepting that our purpose is to serve God is not to grovel in the dust before another human. It is to explore the stars with the Maker of them.

And not only is he the Creator and the Sustainer; he is also the only Savior (**v 36**). Without faith in Jesus, God's wrath remains on us. There is no other way to be saved but through faith in Jesus. This verse sounds very much like **verse 18**: "Whoever believes in him is not condemned, but whoever does not believe stands condemned already because they have not believed in the name of God's one and only Son." How can you possibly avoid a sense of rejoicing when you realize that through faith in Jesus there is "eternal life" (**v 36**)?

In our witness today, while on the one hand we avoid the negative, too often we also avoid the positive. We are not the treasure—we are just jars of clay—but nevertheless we do have treasure
to share (2 Corinthians 4:6). We are not strong—we are weak and
inadequate—but nevertheless there is great power in our witness
(2 Corinthians 4:7). The result of keeping the focus on ourselves is
that we miss all that is on offer to ourselves and to others when we
keep the focus on Christ. He is the Lord of heaven and earth. He
is the Maker of all. By him all things are sustained, and in him and
through faith in him we have life eternal.

Get Out of the Way

Our witness, then, is effective as we get out of the way and point to
Jesus, like John the Witness (and not like his disciples in this story).

That is easier to say than to put into practice! One way to begin to
approach our life and witness this way is to "walk inside" the central
metaphor that John the Witness himself uses to explain his approach.
He is not the bride. He is not the bridegroom. There is a wedding, and
the central event—the wedding of the bride and bridegroom—is not
one in which he is directly involved. But he has an important role to
play. He is "the friend who attends the bridegroom" (John **3:29**)—he
is the best man at the wedding. A best man is "full of joy" as he facili-
tates and witnesses to the main event. Similarly, John is full of joy that
more and more people are turning to Jesus. He does not need to take
center stage; he does not need to be in the limelight. His love for the
Savior is such, and his recognition of the central role that the Savior
must play is so clear, that his joy is full as he sees others recognize Jesus for who he is and begin to follow him. He would not be a witness
if those others were spending their time talking about how wonderful
John the Baptist is. He would have failed in his witness, and would
really only be witnessing to himself, John. Instead, though, they are
following Jesus—and therefore he rejoices.

Much of our witness to Jesus will be freed when we begin to think less about how impressive we are (or how unimpressive we are), less and less about what "they" might think of us, and more and more about Jesus himself and the response of the people to him. That is when we will be effective and joyful—because we will be able to actually, truly, compellingly point others to the Christ.

Questions for reflection

1. Is your own evangelism ever prompted by, or prevented by, a sense of jealousy?

2. How can you make sure that in your life people are aware both that you are a jar of clay, and that you contain gospel treasure (2 Corinthians 4:7)?

3. What will it look like for you to be the friend who attends the bridegroom in your life this week?

PART TWO

The famous story in John 4, of Jesus' encounter with a **Samaritan** woman by a well, is typically preached as an example of evangelistic effectiveness. We look into this narrative and take from it certain techniques for how to reach people—how to have a good introductory question, how to follow up the real need beyond the felt need, how to encourage the interested inquirer to bring others to hear the message, and so on. While no doubt there are elements of this story that are good examples of spreading the good news, the actual intention of this narrative is not first of all to train us in individual evangelism.

To understand John's purpose in telling this particular story, it is important first to notice how he has structured the text. This narrative is formally an "inclusio": it begins with a certain statement, and then it returns to that statement at the end. This is a particular storytelling technique which indicates to the hearer the main point of the narrative. It is easier to spot this sort of approach when we actually listen to the story read: the **oral** nature of this material as read in church often reveals the intentionality in the structure in a way that is sometimes hidden to us when we read it in our heads on our own. When you read the story out loud, you can fairly quickly notice that John begins his story with Jesus leaving for Galilee (**4:3**), and then he ends his story with Jesus arriving at Galilee (**v 43-45**). This story has at its "top" and at its "tail" a Galilee motif. We are listening to a story about what happened to Jesus when he left for Galilee and before he arrived in Galilee.

The Fields are White for Harvest

The top and tail also give another indication of John's main point here. For at the start of the story Jesus is not only leaving for Galilee; he is leaving for Galilee for a particular purpose. The Pharisees—and when this description of this class of individuals is used in John without further elaboration, it is almost always negative in its tone—had heard that Jesus was baptizing more disciples than John (**v 1**). We are meant to wonder immediately: What is this about? Are the Pharisees trying to stir up trouble? Are they fanning flames of jealousy between John's disciples and Jesus' disciples (who were actually the ones doing the baptizing, **v 2**)? There appears to have been some pursuit of Jesus by the Pharisees that caused him to leave for Galilee.

Then at the end of the narrative, in **verse 44**, we find that those from Nazareth, Jesus' "own country" or "hometown," were not liable to accept Jesus either. "A prophet has no honor in his own country," Jesus had said. The Galileans from outside the hometown area of Nazareth did welcome him (**v 45**), but apparently only once they had seen what he had done in Jerusalem. The implicit message is that those from Jesus' home country, as well as the Pharisees, were not predisposed to welcome or accept him.

In **verse 3**, Jesus leaves Judea to go to Galilee and passes through Samaria on his way (**v 4**). Why this route? It is said that the Jews of Jesus' day would avoid traveling through the territory of these **half-caste**, religiously barbaric **heretics**, to avoid hassle, contamination, and danger. The Samaritans were a much-despised group of people who were viewed by the Jerusalem elite as religious **syncretists**, who had compromised with Babylon and opposed the rebuilding of the wall. So Jews would take the longer route round, crossing over the Jordan and traveling through Perea. But Jesus takes the direct route. "He had to go through Samaria." Why? Jesus is making a point. While the Galileans are reluctant followers of Jesus (only susceptible to his influence once he becomes news at the Jerusalem Temple), and while the Pharisees are becoming opposed to Jesus, the Samaritans—the Samaritans of all people!—welcome Jesus.

In other words, this is a lesson in a "strange harvest." This is exactly how Jesus describes the point he wants his disciples to learn:

> "Do you not say, 'There are yet four months, then comes the harvest'? Look, I tell you, lift up your eyes, and see that the fields are white for harvest. Already the one who reaps is receiving wages

and gathering fruit for eternal life, so that sower and reaper may rejoice together. For here the saying holds true, 'One sows and another reaps.' I sent you to reap that for which you did not labor. Others have labored, and you have entered into their labor."

(**v 35-38**, ESV)

Jesus' conclusion is astonishing: "For here the saying holds true." Here? In Samaria? Surely not! And yet, sure enough, "Many of the Samaritans from that town believed in him" (**v 39**). The contrast with the Pharisees and with the hometown is quite startling! What a strange harvest! Yet it is Samaria which accepts Jesus.

To truly grasp the significance of the point that John's narrative is intending to bring out for us, one further piece of information and context is needed: who these Samaritans were. They were despised "half-breeds" from the north of the country who had (the Jews felt) sold out on the true faith and had interbred with non-Jewish people, so that their origin was no longer racially pure, and their religion was compromised.

> Here is the beginning of the New Testament's missionary agenda and promise.

So here in John 4, in other words, is the beginning of the New Testament missionary agenda and promise. The gospel is to go from Jerusalem to Judea to Samaria and to the ends of the earth (Acts 1:8). What is more, Jesus' summary of the meaning of this encounter is intended to show us that this gospel progress is deliberately (and surprisingly) intended to be a strange harvest of great abundance. The gospel is not only for a certain racially pure group. No longer will it be seen as being confined to a particular tribe and nation—now it is, and must be, for all nations. Samaria needs to learn that too, as does Jerusalem, and the ends of the earth.

Living Water and Many Husbands

The rest of the story between these key markers of its message unfolds along lines that are familiar to many of us. But several points need to be underlined. Notice Jesus' willingness to ignore established social norms in order to share the gospel. Jesus, while on his own, speaks on his initiative to a woman on her own at a well (John **4:5-8**). This was not something that Jewish males who wished to remain pure did. As John notes, the woman was surprised because "Jews do not associate with Samaritans" (**v 9**), and especially not with Samaritan women.

It is also important to see the barely-contained humor of the dialogue between Jesus and the woman. Jesus indicates that he has "living water" on offer (**v 10**). Jesus is offering something spiritual to the woman—something of momentous importance. The woman completely misses the point, however, suggesting that Jesus is claiming to be greater than Jacob, who dug the well in the first place (**v 11-12**). Jesus then tries again. One more time he explains that he is talking about a special spiritual drink that leads to eternal life (**v 13-14**). With deadpan humor (or spiritual dullness) the woman still does not apparently get what Jesus is saying (**v 15**). We are witnessing something like an evangelist telling someone they need to believe in order to be saved, and the person thinking that thereby he or she will be able to save more money in their bank account. It is evangelism as spiritual slapstick, worthy of Laurel and Hardy, the Three Stooges, and other renditions of physical or verbal humor like that of Charlie Chaplin.

Next the tables are turned, however. Jesus calls the woman out. "Go, call your husband," he says (**v 16**). The woman (bashfully? Has she been playing along hoping for some seductive subtext in the conversation beforehand?) replies, "I have no husband" (**v 17**). Jesus now employs his sovereign insight and tells her directly about her spiritual situation: she is living a life of **serial monogamy**, working through one husband after another, and she is on her sixth partner (**v 17-18**).

The humor again seems to return in **verse 19**: "Sir ... I can see that you are a prophet." Anyone who has done any pastoral counseling at all will recognize this move. I call it the "punt for theological conversation when all else fails." If the discussion moves a little too close to home, people will sometimes introduce some general topic of theological controversy, hoping that you will forget the point and keep talking about things that have no particular or practical relevance to their lives. And so the woman introduces the age-old debate about whether the Samaritans had to go to Jerusalem, or whether it was okay for them to worship somewhere else other than at the temple (**v 20**)—which is much more comfortable for her than talking about her sex life.

Amazingly, and graciously, Jesus actually replies (**v 21-24**). His reply is serious, and emphasizes the main point of this narrative, which is teaching that there is now a new day when the gospel is going to all nations, and therefore worship does not have to take place in the physical temple in Jerusalem. What God is looking for is true worshipers who will worship "in the Spirit and in truth" (**v 23-24**). "Spirit and truth" is the key variable that is missing from this well-known first-century Jewish-Samaritan theological controversy; the issue is not "place" but "person." Even the "place" of the temple was always intended to be only a vehicle by which the "person" of God could be encountered—the God who revealed himself to Moses and throughout the Old Testament by his personal name, Yahweh, "I AM" (in English Bibles, "the LORD"). And now that I AM has revealed himself in Christ, the "place" is the "person." There can be no physical (geographical) restriction any more. What defines worship is no longer the physical temple.

The woman knows that when the Messiah comes, he will make all these complexities clear (**v 25**) regarding the temple. The Messiah is Jesus himself: "I, the one speaking to you—I am he." Jesus, the I AM, is addressing the woman (**v 26**). Worship from now on is to be worship that is focused upon Jesus as the great I AM; and that is the kind of worship, and the kind of worshippers, that the Father God is seeking. Worshiping "in the Spirit and in truth," means people from all nations and all places worshiping the person of Jesus himself, who is the truth to whom the Spirit points.

A Clean Sheet in a New Land

At this point in the interaction, Jesus' disciples return, and John delicately indicates that though they are surprised, they do not ask him any questions (**v 27**). For a woman to be alone at this well at this hour of the day was highly irregular. And for Jesus to be engaging her in personal conversation was particularly unusual. They are, as the British would say, gobsmacked; they are left speechless. They can't even mumble a question, though they must have a whole host of questions running through their heads.

The woman's response, however, is quite different. She is not speechless; rather, she is full of speech! She goes home and spreads the good news (**v 28-29**). Soon enough, this loose-living woman becomes a most effective evangelist, and scores of people come out of the town to see Jesus for themselves (**v 30**). Who is this Person?

The disciples, meanwhile, miss the point (**v 31**). They decide that Jesus must be hungry (after all, wasn't he thirsty? He had just been asking for a drink, had he not?), and so Jesus tries to redirect them to understand what is actually going on (**v 32-34**). Just as the woman had thought it was about water (when really it was about the water of life), so the disciples thought it was about food (when really it was about the message of Jesus going forward, even to Samaria).

Then Jesus uses his harvest **analogy** (**v 35-38**), a familiar one of the end times and the harvest that is to come. What is shocking about this is that Jesus says the harvest is here, at this moment—that is, in Samaria, in this gospel outreach! "For here the saying holds true," (**v 37**, ESV). And Jesus is right: the Samaritan villagers come to hear Jesus because of the woman's witness (**v 39**); they ask him to stay (**v 40**); and they believe because of Jesus' teaching (**v 41-42**).

We are never given the name of this "Samaritan woman." Perhaps John is carefully maintaining her anonymity in order to preserve her against any acute embarrassment, as Jesus has so publicly diagnosed her life of sinfulness before she followed Jesus. Now she has been for-given, she is starting a new life, and she has a clean sheet—all that is in the past stays in the past, and her shame is now gone. This woman of Samaria is now a follower of Jesus, because Jesus has held out the gospel to her as he has engaged with her:

> "Through the entire conversation Jesus deals with [the Samaritan woman] as a person in her own right, with her unique history and special longings. She emerges in the account as a credible character with personal dignity—because Jesus treats her as such. Simply put, Jesus loved her and was prepared to breach age-old conventions to reach her." (Milne, *John,* page 86)

The Strange Harvest

So here it is: the harvest. In Samaria (of all places!). Jesus offers a kind of first "I AM" statement (**v 26**—literally, he says here, "I am who is speaking to you"), and is for the first time proclaimed by others not just as a rabbi but as the "Savior of the world" (**v 42**). A strange harvest—a harvest of strangers, of foreigners, of the nations.

Perhaps you are tempted, like the woman, to put up various verbal defenses against the all-too-close approach of Jesus. Maybe there are some aspects of your life that you would not like to have brought out into the open or examined too carefully—especially not by those pesky religious disciples of Jesus! Take this moment to meet with Jesus your-self through faith and in prayer. Listen to his approach through his word by his Spirit. He is the water of life that you need. Nothing else will satisfy, only him, and his satisfaction is forever, so that we are constantly filled and have a spring of living water flowing from within.

Do we experience this "living water"? It is a question that we must face. This is not mechanical engagement with religion or church but a personal relationship with Jesus. Is this your experience of God? Would you ask Jesus to increasingly give you his living water, his Spirit?

Do we worship in the Spirit and in truth? Is our worship together filled with truth about God—not empty-headed, meaningless, vacuous, content-less vagueness, but thoughtful, God-centered truth, which causes us to reflect upon and reflect outwards the truth of the gospel? And is our worship at the same time "Spiritual"—that is, not merely human-level, not just worked-up human emotions, but an actual relational bowing down, by God's Spirit, before God himself, in love and in adoration? Let us ask God to meet us by his Spirit, so that we might worship him in truth and Spirit.

Questions for reflection

1. Are there any ways in which you unconsciously (or consciously) assume the gospel is only for people who are like you, be that ethnically, culturally or economically?

2. "What defines worship is no longer the physical temple." What are the implications of this truth for your church building?

3. Are there areas of your life that you would like to pretend Jesus does not see, because you are pursuing something else to give you satisfaction? What would drinking living water mean for you?

5. JESUS RULES

The real drama of life is so often personal.

Sometimes a well-known individual behaves in public in a way that surprises us, or causes us to wonder what is really going on in their personal lives. Very often our public actions, our workplace interactions, or our committee interventions are interfered with and affected by our private state—not just the state of our heart (though "out of ... the heart the mouth speaks"—Matthew 12:34, ESV) but also by our family life, and the concerns of our friends and those closest to us.

It would be easy for us to think that a "royal official" (John **4:46**) would need little by way of encouragement or healing. But then we discover that his son is sick, and seriously unwell. Jesus is not immune to such encounters with sick people or people in difficulties, and here he meets a man who, though powerful, is also powerless: he fears his child will die (**v 49**). Those of us who have had sick sons or daughters, who perhaps have even buried a child, will know the almost unbearable pain that is behind those few words. And here Jesus meets with him.

A Desperate Man

Jesus is now re-entering Cana of Galilee, the place (John reminds us) where Jesus had turned water into wine (**v 46**). The significance, literally, of that reminder is that now Jesus will perform his second sign in this place (**v 54**). This time, however, it is not a wedding which provides the context for Jesus' miraculous sign, but a lone individual with a sick child (**v 46**). John does not tell us the name of the "official" who made the journey from Capernaum to Cana to see Jesus, hoping that he would heal his child; we are only told that he is some kind of official, which in all likelihood meant that he was a royal official in **King Herod's** service. This was a person of administrative responsibilities, perhaps of high standing, which is why his journey to see the true King Jesus was of such note to John, and why he recorded it so carefully. It is possible, too, that as a man in Herod's service he was a Gentile, which as Köstenberger highlights, would have been significant too:

> "If this man was a Gentile, then this marks a progression from Jew (John 3) to Samaritan to Gentile (John 4) in Jesus' ministry, in keeping with the pattern followed also in the Book of Acts (1:8)." (*John*, page 169)

It is worth taking a moment to imagine the scene, so that we can begin to grasp the desperate human need and the dramatic nature of the sign that is to come. We have here a person of high standing, an officer, likely in the dubious royal service of King Herod. He may come with fanfare, he may have money, he may have power, but he also has a sick child. We are privileged to see the news behind the news. This person perhaps had a public profile (is that why in this story he is just an "official" and remains unnamed?) and a reputation of some standing and honor. Such people often look as though they are able to skim over the surface of more normal human suffering, dining on success and feasting on favor; yet here he is with a sick child. The human condition is breaking through into the life of this official.

What's more, as we complete our imagined profile, this child is not just sick; he is "close to death" (John **4:47**). The man is desperate. His beloved son is about to die. He has lost all hope. He hears of the latest traveling quack doctor offering supernatural remedies; he calls together his retinue and in haste he makes the journey. All other doctors have failed him. Will this Jesus also fail him?

Jesus' reply, given the drama of this official's arrival and the personal story that he carried with him, is astonishing. Jesus seems to be operating on a theological level while the official is simply concerned about the fact that his son is dying. Jesus says, "Unless you people see signs and wonders … you will never believe" (**v 48**). Is this a rebuke? Is it a statement of fact?

We need to pause here to consider the somewhat ambivalent usage of signs in John's Gospel. John, in his purpose statement for the whole Gospel in 20:30-31, makes it clear that Jesus' signs are intended to give us reason to believe. Signs, therefore, have a God-given, positive purpose in John's Gospel; they are so "that you may believe." However, in this instance in John 4, there appears to be a wisp of longing on Jesus' part for a world in which those signs are not necessary. "Unless you people see signs and wonders … you will never believe" (**4:48**) seems equivalent to a desire that Jesus would be taken and trusted on his own, without the need for the fireworks of miraculous displays of supernaturally impressive wonders. Further, here we see that Jesus uses every instance to teach. Yes, signs are given that we may believe. No, we are not to rely on the signs. We are to rely on Jesus himself. As Jesus will later say to **doubting Thomas**, "Blessed are those who have not seen and yet have believed" (20:29). Even though signs are provided in John's Gospel, it is better to believe without signs and to believe on the basis of the word. As Paul says, "Faith comes from hearing the message, and the message is heard through the word about Christ" (Romans 10:17).

A Desperate Prayer

The royal official responds to Jesus by again appealing for help: "Sir, come down before my child dies" (John **4:49**). He is not interested in the theological niceties of the right way to show faith; we might wonder whether, or to what extent, he is even at this point interested in Jesus himself! Yet Jesus answers his prayer: "Go … your son will live" (**v 50**). Note, though, how John immediately realizes that genuine faith is at work in the official, even if it is superficial, orientated toward his own personal need, and not fully fledged. "The man took Jesus at his word and departed" (**v 50**).

Is there a lesson here for those of us who tend to ask too much of potential converts? It is certainly true that mature faith should realize that Jesus himself is the greatest reward—but this man senses Jesus' ability to help, comes to Jesus for the healing of his son, and believes Jesus' word, and Jesus chooses to answer his desperate prayer. Can we make it harder for people to come to Christ than Christ himself did, by asking of them a level of maturity which is unreasonable to expect of a young Christian, let alone a desperate seeker after healing? How could we learn from Jesus' willingness to accept this official's prayer, despite it not being couched in the required terminology of the rabbinic schools? Would we correct someone who came to us to say that they wanted to believe in Jesus because they had a sick child and they had heard that Jesus was a great healer? Jesus does not correct, though he does speak of the need to respond in belief—he heals the son.

I wonder also whether there is a lesson for our prayer life. This is the passionate, intemperate, insistent prayer of a desperate man. Are our prayers too polite? The man comes to Jesus, appeals to Jesus, and he is heard by Jesus. Could we learn from this to pray more passionately, more desperately, more insistently? Certainly, we have no guarantee that every sick child in this world will be healed. Unless Christ comes first, we will all at some point die. But we do have the promise that he hears us when we pray (1 John 5:15), even if his answer now is "only" to provide us with the ongoing strength that we need to meet the difficulties that we face. "You do not have because you do not ask God," James points out to members of the early church (James 4:2). The royal official could not be accused of that, and neither should we be.

Your Hour of Need

The story continues: the man leaves, goes home, and is met by his servants (John **4:51**). Clearly, this is a man of some significance. When they tell him at what time his son was healed (**v 52**), he realizes that it was at that precise moment that Jesus gave the word for him to be healed (**v 53**). It is so encouraging to think that Jesus does not have to be physically present to have an impact on us, but that we can receive his ministry simply through the power of his word—at a distance, as it were. Without him having to be next to us in body, he can be next to us in Spirit, and his word can still have a powerful healing, saving, encouraging impact.

Once more we are told that the official believed, and now not just him but "his whole household" (**v 53**). Perhaps he believed even more now that he saw the power of Jesus' word. Perhaps his faith increased. Perhaps this realization, that it was at the precise moment when Jesus spoke that his son was healed, began to show him just who this Jesus truly was. F.F. Bruce describes his experience neatly:

"Life, almost extinguished in the battle with death, had suddenly gained new strength from Jesus' reviving word and won the victory." (*The Gospel of John,* page 257)

His faith was growing, because he was beginning to get a bigger sense of who Jesus was. A fledgling disciple, to be sure, and one about whom we know precious little (and nothing further after this episode). But what John does tell us is that an "official" and his whole household, slaves as well as family, were brought to follow Jesus. All because of a sick son, a desperate father, and a compassionate Jesus.

> Every sickness can be transformed into something purposeful and meaningful.

Perhaps you have some great sadness in your life. It could be a sick child. It could be a sick spouse, or a broken relationship. This side of glory not every sickness is healed. But every sickness can be transformed into something purposeful, meaningful, a place of significance through the work of Christ, and from the perspective of God's sovereignty. As Paul says, God interweaves all things for his glory and for our good (Romans 8:28); this is at times supremely hard to believe. Which is why, in prayer, we need to go to God and meet with him, to encounter Christ, to relate to him personally, and to hear his word to us through the Scriptures. We need to put ourselves in a place where we can be reminded of his power and his compassion—in a place where Christ can encourage us, give perspective to us, and meet us in our hour of need. That's what enables us to believe Christ, so that, again or for the first time, we and our whole household, our family and our friends, our business colleagues and our network of connections can see the difference in how we act and live as a result of the fact that we have met with Jesus, and he has reached out to us, and his word has brought healing to us.

Perhaps you know someone who, though powerful, has difficulties in their lives. They may be a "royal official," but they are not able to overcome that addiction, or that sense of failure or insecurity, or they do not know how to get their life back on track after that family tragedy. Perhaps you could bring them to this very passage of Scripture, and ask them to believe in the Jesus who can renew them, and at a word heal them, and give them fresh hope, meaning, and purpose, for his glory and for their good.

Questions for reflection

1. What would you say to someone who said, "I'd believe in Jesus if he did a miracle right in front of me"?

2. In what circumstances in your own life do you find it hard to believe that God could be at work? How does this story encourage you?

3. Are there people of whom you only see their prestige or power, but not their spiritual need? What would change if you remembered that few are without difficulties and no one is without sin?

PART TWO

Sabbath Rules... or Jesus Rules?

Now begins the transition in Jesus' relationship with the Pharisees. Before this, they had been interested and inquisitive, albeit sometimes suspicious, observers of what he was doing and saying. The cleansing of the temple (2:13-22) had tested the religious elite's patience to the extreme, causing the Jewish authorities to ask him for a special miraculous sign of his authority to do such an outrageous deed (v 18). His answer, that he was going to destroy this temple and then rebuild it in three days, cannot have helped matters, even though it sounded so enigmatic that his meaning was presumably as lost to them as it was to his disciples. The Pharisees were probably stirring up trouble when they pointed out that Jesus was getting more of a following than John the Baptist (4:1). And it's possible that, given the association between Herod's household and the Sadducees—the religious competitors of the Pharisees—Jesus' healing of the official's son may not have helped his reputation with them. But now, in this passage, Jesus crosses the line.

From Observers to Enemies

As we'll see, Jesus appears to break the Sabbath rules which Pharisaical tradition mandated, and not only does he break those rules but he then explains that he is doing so because in fact he is in charge of everything, including the Sabbath, making himself equal with God. At this point, the Pharisees move from being observers to enemies.

So here is Jesus' "crossing the Rubicon" moment. As Julius Caesar in ancient history decided when the moment came to cross the northern boundary of the area around Rome into which no army was allowed—the River Rubicon—so Jesus now crosses a boundary and is viewed as invading the territory belonging to God alone. This is· the point of no return, and so intense is their resulting animosity that the Pharisees "tried all the more to kill him" (**5:18**). At its essence, this passage is about a choice—a choice between religious rules as defined by humans within certain mandated religious systems or the rule of King Jesus himself.

The story begins with another feast (**v 1**): "Some time later, Jesus went up to Jerusalem for one of the Jewish festivals." It is not clear exactly which feast is in consideration, and different opinions have been offered. Some think it was the Feast of Trumpets. The bottom line is that we do not know, and John does not make it clear, so specifying exactly which feast is clearly not essential to the meaning of this story, or for applying it to our lives. There was another major gathering, like one of our Christian conferences, and Jesus went up to be a part of it.

This time, however, the story plays out not in the temple but in a place that was visited by the sick. There was a particular pool called Bethesda (**v 2**), where people who were invalids would come hoping to find healing (**v 3**). Apparently there was a lot of popular mythology about this pool; in most modern English translations, **verse 4** is put into a footnote because most scholars do not think that it belonged to the original text. Even if this verse was not in the original, however, it shows that there was a well-known popular hope that this particular pool was the place where God would heal individuals.

Imagine a world where there is no modern medicine. Imagine all the sick and the lame, the blind and the diseased, and imagine the hope that a particular place, a special pool, can provide healing. Perhaps it really was true that an angel would at times come and disturb the pool and bring healing. We do not know. We do know that invalids believed that it was true, and Jesus apparently seems to feel no need to correct this popular myth.

In **verse 5**, John introduces us to one particular man, "who had been an invalid for thirty-eight years." By anyone's reckoning, this is an extremely extended period in which to suffer, and even today it would cause significant pain, and might lead to bitterness and anger as well. Jesus sees him lying there, and whether by divine insight or because someone present told him, he "learned that he had been in this condition for a long time" (**v 6**).

Jesus asks him very simply, "Do you want to get well?" It is a strange question—why else was the invalid there unless he wanted to be healed?! Why would anyone go to a hospital, find someone who is seriously sick, and has been for a long time, and ask them whether they want to get better? It could be that Jesus wondered whether the man's lengthy illness, and the lack of any progress in recovery, had led him to the point where he needed stirring up into action: *Don't you want to get better?* Perhaps Jesus is provoking in the man any last vestiges of faith that God can heal him—a faith that surely has been tested after thirty-eight years of waiting.

The man replies in **verse 7** that the reason why he is just lying there is because he has no one to help him down into the healing pools at exactly the right time when the water is "stirred," apparently the point at which those who are put in will be healed. The human condition is exposed further. Not only is this man a long-term invalid, but although he lies right next to the (apparent) medicine, he has no one who will actually take him the few steps further to receive it. Who brought him to this pool? Why did they not stay to take him into the water? The man appears to be not just an invalid physically, but also to be relationally incapacitated—alone and friendless.

His faith in the magical properties of the pool may be misplaced, or perhaps people really were healed there. Presumably something wholesome happened; otherwise, it would not have gained its repu-tation. But within moments, the man has no further need of hope in or help from the pool: "Then Jesus said to him, 'Get up! Pick up your mat and walk.' At once the man was cured; he picked up his mat and walked" (**v 8-9**). Notice the sheer, stark contrast between the endless wait for an unlikely healing from some stirred-up water and the simple divine command of Jesus! Jesus speaks; it is so.

You're Well... But Take Care

But this miracle brings us to Jesus' Rubicon: the Sabbath. Suddenly we hear why it is that John has included this particular story about Jesus (for John was very selective in the material he chose to include in his book—see 21:25). "The day on which this took place was a Sabbath" (**5:9**). In case we miss the significance of that "bridge" which Jesus has now crossed, John explains by means of the conversation that the Jewish leaders had with the man who had been healed: "It is the Sabbath; the law forbids you to carry your mat" (**v 10**).

Some further explanation is helpful. The Jewish leaders had learned the lesson of the Babylonian exile almost too well. Having been sent into exile for breaking the Sabbath, worshiping idols, and not following God's law, they now were determined to make sure that not the slightest infraction was committed in case it led to a fresh exile (Leviticus 26:43). They had become the Sabbath police. Rules that were intended to guard against working on a Sabbath, to proclaim the higher meaning of the Sabbath as a rest in God (itself to be fulfilled in Jesus— see Matthew 12:8), had become oppressive burdens that prevented a man from being healed on a Sabbath! So they accosted the man for breaking a stipulation related to "work" on the Sabbath (Exodus 16:29), which they no doubt viewed as potentially extremely serious (Numbers 15:32), and likely to provoke a repeat of Israel's history that they were determined to avoid (Jeremiah 17:21-22).

Faced with this religious authority accusing him of what could be a serious crime, the man punts the problem to a higher authority (John **5:11**). He was only doing what someone else—"the man who made [him] well"—had told him to do. Immediately, the focus of attention (and threat) turns from the man who has been made well to this man who made him well (**v 12**).

We may wonder whether the man who had been healed by Jesus did a particularly good job at bearing witness! At one level his ignorance is understandable for he did not know who had healed him, because Jesus had withdrawn as there was a crowd present (**v 13**).

But could he not have responded in a way that was more obviously appreciative of the fact that he had been healed? Certainly, we will see that a man who was born blind, when healed by Jesus, answers his accusers with far more vim, verve, and vigor (9:30-33). It was understandable for this invalid to avoid accusation, but when called to give an account for why he was doing something which previously he had been unable to do, it would not be beyond the bounds of normal gratitude to mention his healing with appreciation, even in that context. And if the man had grasped something of who had healed him, and the higher meaning of this healing, then his witness could have been more vigorous and committed still.

Our instinct—that the man has not understood much if any of the spiritual dimensions of his healing, let alone expressed basic human appreciation—is confirmed by his next interaction with Jesus in **5:14**. "Later Jesus found him at the temple and said to him, 'See, you are well again. Stop sinning or something worse may happen to you.'" We know that physical ailments are not always the direct result of particular sins (though all suffering and pain in this world is the general result of the fallen nature of this world). Jesus will make this principle clear in 9:3, where he says clearly that the blind man's healing is necessary, not because the blind man has sinned, nor because his parents have sinned, but because the situation is part of God's design to show his glory by healing him. Not all difficulty or suffering is the direct result of an individual's particular sin.

However, sometimes suffering and pain is the direct result of a particular sin. And in this instance it was. Jesus had healed him of suffering and pain that had somehow been connected to his own sin, and Jesus now warns him to stop sinning, otherwise something worse will happen to him. What was his sin? We are not told, but if the foregoing account is anything to go by, it may have been deep spiritual ingratitude. He did not mention his appreciation for having been healed at all. Is it by chance that when Jesus first came across him he was alone, and that while someone was willing to take him to the pool, no one was willing to take him down into the pool to be healed? Was he the sort of person who drove other people away because he would not say "thank you" and mean it, and therefore he was living a life of relational incapacity as much as physical incapacity? We do not know, but the man comes across as someone who is fixated on himself rather than other people, let alone remembering God and worshiping him in joy and gratitude.

The "something worse" that Jesus says will happen to him if he does not stop sinning is not clearly defined (**5:14**). John does not explain Jesus' enigmatic statement, but it is likely that Jesus' warning is that this man has been healed once; if he keeps on with his life of sin, he might come to the point where no more healing will be given, and all that will be left will be the judgment that John's Gospel has already warned is the result of rejecting Jesus (3:36).

His brief conversation with Jesus now over, the man goes away and tells the Jewish leaders that it was Jesus who had healed him (**5:15**). So the Jewish leaders now turn their attack directly upon Jesus (**v 16**). Jesus' answer to their accusations in **verse 17** is fascinating because, far from ameliorating or downplaying their concerns, it raises the stakes significantly. Think what Jesus could have chosen to say in his defense. He could have argued that the Old Testament nowhere said that it was wrong to do good on the Sabbath. He could have argued that the man was not "working" on the Sabbath by carrying his bed, but was instead witnessing to what God had done in his life, and therefore he was "worshiping," not working. But if Jesus argued like that, he would be operating within the constraints of the Old Testament and under its authority. What Jesus had done was within the constraints of the law, and that case could certainly have been made. However, Jesus himself was not under the authority of the law, but was the Author himself. This is why Jesus responds to their opposition in the way he does in **verse 17**: "In his defense Jesus said to them, 'My Father is always at his work to this very day, and I too am working.'"

In rabbinic Judaism a discussion had developed regarding whether it could be said that God stopped working entirely on the Sabbath.

Genesis 2:3 says that God did rest on the Sabbath—but what sort of "rest" was this? Surely, if God entirely ceased from all activity on one day in seven, then the universe itself would cease to exist for one day in seven. The Jewish scholars concluded, then, that while God did indeed rest on the Sabbath, this was not a rest of completely ceasing from activity but rather a rest from the original creation act, and a symbolic rest that indicated that this day was special. So it was not wrong to say that God was always working.

Jesus picks up on this conclusion when he says, "My Father is always at his work" and adds that, in the same way, he is always working too (**v 17**). This is a quite extraordinary claim. Jesus is arguing that what he has done is evidence that he is equal with God. As Carson points out:

> "For this self-defense to be valid, the same factors that apply to God must apply to Jesus: either he is above the law given to mere mortals, or, if he operates within the law, it is because the entire universe is his." (John, page 247)

The Jewish leaders will prove to be spiritually blind—but they are not stupid. They fully understand what Jesus is saying: "He was even calling God his own Father, making himself equal with God" (**v 18**). Therefore, they consider him to be a heretic, **blasphemous**, and worthy of death.

One lesson that we should learn from the Jewish leaders here is that it is easier than any of us will want to admit to refashion truly biblical commitments into restrictive, human-centered tokens of pride and communal distinction. Legalism is

> It is easy to refashion biblical commitments into restrictive tokens of pride.

not, of course, to be confused with discipline. To be disciplined is like being well trained for playing a game of tennis; to be legalistic is like creating a set of rules so that only certain very special people (who happen to include ourselves) can play tennis at all. Are there religious rules that we have made legalistic (not merely matters of discipline)? If so, the answer, and the real point of this story, is to come to Jesus himself as fully God and find our hope, healing, and salvation in personal relationship with him, and not in any religious rules.

Questions for reflection

1. "It is easier than any of us will want to admit to refashion truly biblical commitments into restrictive human-centered tokens of pride and communal distinction." Does your church culture elevate particular rules—perhaps made for very good reasons—above loving and serving Jesus?

2. Are you in any danger of living with spiritual ingratitude? What would your prayer life suggest as the answer to that question?

3. Has your view of the link between sin and suffering been changed in any way by this section?

6. IS JESUS REALLY GOD?

The question, "Is Jesus really God?" is one that is regularly asked today. People find it hard to accept the claim that Jesus, a man born at a certain time and place, could also be the God of the whole universe incarnate. Our understanding of the sheer scale of the cosmos, and the magnitude and complexity of reality, means that it is difficult to conceptualize the One who made all of that and keeps it running as also a man who walked around Galilee a couple of thousand years ago.

However, as hard as people today find it to accept that Jesus is really, truly God, it was far harder for people then. Imagine what it must have been like for a first-century Jew, belonging to the most vigorously **monotheistic** people the world had ever seen, to process the claim that the man standing in front of them was equal to God the Father. But this was exactly what Jesus was claiming in **verse 18**. This verse sets the trajectory of the whole discourse that we are looking at in this chapter. The Jewish leaders rightly understood the claims that Jesus was making about himself, even though they were horrified by them—so, John comments:

> "For this reason they tried all the more to kill him [that is, Jesus];
> not only was he breaking the Sabbath, but he was even calling
> God his own Father, making himself equal with God." (**v 18**)

This claim was a bridge too far for many of the Jewish leaders at the time. It is not hard to see why what Jesus was saying stuck in their throats. They had been taught to believe in one God. The well-known *Shema* of Israel puts it like this: "Hear, O Israel: The LORD our God, the LORD is one" (Deuteronomy 6:4).

This monotheism was not a mere theoretical abstraction, like some of the higher philosophies of ancient Greece. This was a full-orbed personal, radical commitment to the total oneness of God, the worship of him, and the defense of this proposition.

Jewish monotheism was a radical commitment to the total oneness of God.

This idea of God being "one" was simply hardwired into the Jewish mindset by this time. A couple of events had made it firm in their heads, even if sometimes beforehand they had wavered in this commitment. In particular, the Babylonian exile, from which the Jewish people had only relatively recently returned, had been caused by their idolatry—their worship of other gods. 2 Kings 17:7-23, referring to the earlier invasion by the Assyrians (which resulted in the northern part of the land that God had given his people being conquered) makes this connection between God's people losing sight of God being one, embracing idolatry, and going into exile:

"All this took place because the Israelites had sinned against the LORD their God, who had brought them up out of Egypt from under the power of Pharaoh king of Egypt. They worshiped other gods... They worshiped idols... So the people of Israel were taken from their homeland into exile in Assyria..." (v 7, 12, 23)

This was in fulfillment of what God had promised would happen if they forgot that God was the only God, and forgot to worship him alone:

"Then the LORD will scatter you among all nations, from one end of the earth to the other. There you will worship other gods— gods of wood and stone, which neither you nor your ancestors have known." (Deuteronomy 28:64)

This background of exile because of idolatry is important to bear in mind when we consider the violent response of Israel's leadership to

Jesus' claim to be equal to God. As far as they could see, it appeared that Jesus was about to try to lead God's people astray all over again. They had learned from the exile what God would do if they became idolatrous, and they were not about to let that happen again. They were therefore zealously opposed to Jesus because he claimed to be equal to God.

So, hard as some people today find it to accept that Jesus is God, it was indubitably far harder for Israel's leaders to accept it. They were passionately monotheistic, whereas our culture today is **relativistically** non-committal. The response of people today to Jesus' claim to be God is an unbelieving but unbothered shrug (as long as that faith is kept private); the response then was a murderous opposition.

Jesus' reply is a winning riposte to those who had grown up within a passionate but simplistic monotheism that refused to accept that God, and not his people, is the One who is authoritatively able to describe his own nature. And it may well also contain an effective response for our more relativistic culture today.

Nine Reasons Jesus' Divinity is Common Sense

In John **5:19-47**, Jesus only really makes two points. The first (**verses 19-29**) is regarding who he is in essence. Then, from **verses 30-47**, Jesus shows that not only does the proposition of him being equal to Father God make good sense in principle, but it is also a proposition for which there is good evidence. Let's look, then, at these two answers to the question "Is Jesus really God?" (the first in this part; the second in part two).

The first answer is: Jesus' equality with God the Father neither diminishes the "Godness" of the Father nor the "Godness" of Jesus. So it isn't nonsensical to believe that Jesus is God. Jesus gives nine reasons why his divinity is defensible by **sanctified** common sense:

1. Jesus and the Father are inextricably intertwined in their activity. Jesus puts it like this: "Very truly I tell you, the Son can do nothing

by himself; he can do only what he sees his Father doing, because whatever the Father does the Son also does" (**v 19**). The point Jesus is making is that we should not think that saying Jesus and God the Father are equal means that they have different zones of activity, while still somehow remaining equal. Jesus is claiming that what he does, the Father does, and what the Father does, Jesus does. This is a kind of equality that is essential in nature and not merely compatible.

2. The bond between the Father and the Son is love. Jesus tells them that "the Father loves the Son and shows him all he does" (**v 20a**). This truth—that the bond between the Father and the Son is love—has led theologians from Augustine to **Jonathan Edwards** to theorize that the means of communication of love between the Father and the Son is essentially the Holy Spirit. Jesus does not explicitly make that point here, though he may suggest that idea. Here Jesus is saying that the proposition that he and the Father are one is believable because their unity is held together by the deepest possible commitment: love.

3. Jesus indicates that the miracles he has been doing prove he is equal with God the Father, and that there is more evidence of this nature to come: "He [the Father] will show him [the Son] even greater works than these, so that you will be amazed" (**v 20b**). These "greater works" are works related to the signs that Jesus has completed (the third sign being the healing at the pool in verses 1-15, which has created the current conflict between Jesus and the Jewish religious leaders). Jesus is essentially saying, *You ain't seen nothing yet!* There will be even greater signs to come that will show who he is.

4. Jesus says that the greatest power imaginable is equally his as well as the Father's. "For just as the Father raises the dead and gives them life, even so the Son gives life to whom he is pleased to give it" (**v 21**). Jesus will prove this later when he rises from the dead. The point here is that we are not to think that part, but

not all, of God the Father's almighty power is invested in Jesus. No, the whole power of God is invested in Jesus thoroughly and completely, even resurrection power—as John's Gospel will show soon enough (see pages 181-182).

5. Jesus not only has the greatest power imaginable, but he also has the most fearful role imaginable: "Moreover, the Father judges no one, but has entrusted all judgment to the Son" (**v 22**). We tend to think of God the Father judging (and **verse 19** tells us that is not wrong), but we do not tend to think of Jesus as our Judge. Yet, when the day of judgment comes, Jesus will judge. Right here, Jesus is raising the stakes against his opponents. He is showing them that when they think he is saying he is equal to God the Father, they are right to think that is what he is saying! He is specifying each controversial implication, and making sure that they understand that he means every possible one. He is fully and completely equal with the Father.

6. Jesus shows them that his equality with the Father means that the way they treat him shows how they are truly treating God the Father. Jesus says that those who really worship God will respond to him by "honor[ing] the Son just as they honor the Father. Whoever does not honor the Son does not honor the Father, who sent him" (**v 23**). This means that the one thing we cannot say is that we know God, love God, or honor God, if we do not know Jesus, love Jesus, and honor Jesus. Whatever God we are worshiping, if we oppose Jesus, the God we worship is not God the Father and is not the true God.

7. Jesus shows that his word is as powerful as the word of God the Father. Jesus says:

> "Very truly I tell you, whoever hears my word and believes him who sent me has eternal life and will not be judged but has crossed over from death to life. Very truly I tell you, a time is coming and has now come when the dead will

hear the voice of the Son of God and those who hear will live." (**v 24-25**)

Not only what Jesus does but what Jesus says has the power of God. That power is invested in Jesus' word.

8. Jesus uses language about life that reminds us that John's Prologue, with its statement about Jesus being God, is an articulation of what Jesus himself said. Jesus puts it like this: "For as the Father has life in himself, so he has granted the Son also to have life in himself" (**v 26**). This reminds us of 1:4: "In him was life, and that life was the light of all mankind." Jesus, then, not only gives life, and not only has words of life, but he has life in his own being. He is the author of life.

9. Jesus refers again to the day of judgment, indicating that actually the issue is not our judgment of him, but his judgment of us. For the first time in John's Gospel, he refers to himself as "the Son of Man." The "Son of Man" was a mysterious figure of divine power and authority described in Daniel in the Old Testament (see Daniel 7:13-14). Jesus uses this figure of the "Son of Man" to indicate that his essence as authority and God himself was predicted and taught in the Old Testament. He puts it like this:

> "And he [the Father] has given him authority to judge because he is the Son of Man. Do not be amazed at this, for a time is coming when all who are in their graves will hear his voice and come out—those who have done what is good will rise to live, and those who have done what is evil will rise to be condemned." (John **5:27-29**)

The phrases "done what is good" and "done what is evil" suggest to us a moralistic approach to salvation—that we are saved entirely based upon our moral actions or "good works." But Jesus has already taught in **verse 24** that salvation comes from hearing his word and believing the One who sent Jesus, and he will teach a variation of the same point in **verse 40**. In this context, "doing what is good" equals faith in Jesus. This is strange to our ears, because of our association of "do-ing good" with the "good deeds" that are contrasted with "faith" else-where in the New Testament, but Jesus makes the connection plain in 6:29: "The work of God is this: to believe in the one he has sent." Real faith in Jesus is itself the work that God requires; and such faith, when genuine, bears fruit in practical obedience to Jesus too.

> Real faith in Jesus is the work that God requires.

Who's Judging Whom?

Having finished his description of his essence as fully equal with God the Father, Jesus turns the tables on those who were judging him for making what they considered to be such an outrageous claim. *Oh no,* Jesus is saying. *It is I who will judge you, and not the other way around.*

Such a "turning of the tables" is as necessary today as it was then. Many of us tend to approach God from the perspective of our own desires and needs. It is hard for us to make the leap to ask instead, "What does Jesus think of me?" rather than "What do I think of Jesus?" But that is the correct starting point: What is God's assessment of what is best for me? What is God's view of what is the best life for me to pursue? What is God's view of what is sinful and what is beautiful? Instead of trying to fit Jesus into my already-formed preferences—squeezing him into the corners of my self-con-structed lifestyle and relativistic approach to questions of faith and the divine—I am called to bow before him, center my life upon him, and joyfully submit to him.

Questions for reflection

Which of Jesus' nine points about his own identity do you find:

1. new for you?

2. most encouraging for your own faith?

3. most helpful for speaking with and challenging those you know who think Jesus is not God?

PART TWO

The Evidential Defense

For many, the argument that Jesus is merely a "good teacher" seems persuasive—until, that is, they come face to face with Jesus himself. In choosing our response to his claim to be God, we face the famous "trilemma" set out by C.S. Lewis: are we going to view Jesus as Lord, liar, or lunatic? Given that Jesus' life and his teaching make it very hard to rationally conclude that he was either a liar or a lunatic, the only logical alternative is that he is who he claimed to be. Jesus' claims to be the Lord are startling enough; they are also expressed in a way that is consistent with a monotheistic view of God (as we saw in the previous section), and further, they are based on evidence—the evidence that is found in a number of witnesses to Jesus' nature as God (which is the focus of this section).

Call the Witnesses

The discourse that began in **4:19** continues. Jesus, having made the case that his divinity is holistically consistent with biblical principles of monotheism, now argues that there are also evidential reasons for believing that he is God.

First, Jesus had argued, monotheists can believe that he really is God because his equality with God the Father neither diminishes the "Godness" of the Father nor the "Godness" of Jesus (v 19-29).

Now second, Jesus shows that his claim to be equal with God the Father is verifiable and defensible because of the witnesses that he describes (**v 30-47**). As Milne puts it:

"We are not concerned here with a bare monotheism but with a rich trinitarianism. This unique interrelationship of revealing and imitating is rooted in the mutual love of Father and Son. Thus the revelation of God in the Son is finally grounded, not only in the love of God for the world—a love which moves the Father to impart himself to sinners—but also in the eternal love of the Father for the Son—a love which moves the Father to reveal his deeds to the Son. This is holy ground indeed."

(*John*, page 98)

Having established that his claim to be equal with God the Father is indeed intellectually defensible, Jesus now takes his rebuttal to those who are criticizing him for being one with the Father an extra step further.

To begin with, Jesus makes it clear that he is not going to rely on himself, in the sense of rebelling against his Father God, but that he seeks the will of him who sent him (**v 30**). Jesus does not say that his witness to himself is not proper; if Jesus is who he says he is, then surely no other witness could be greater, for what could be a greater witness than the witness of God! However, for the sake of those he is trying to reach, Jesus does not rely upon the principle that, since he is God, he alone can accurately witness to who he is. He points to witnesses that God has given within their reach that should persuade them of who he is.

That is why Jesus says in **verse 31**, "If I testify about myself, my testimony is not true." Jesus is not saying that his own witness is not intellectually or theoretically or actually true in itself (of course it is true; what could be more true than the witness of God?), but he understands that if he alone witnesses to himself, those who are listening are less likely to believe that such a witness is true in practice. They will not think that that witness is trustworthy.

So Jesus presents "another" witness (**v 32**). In fact, he will present four. The first witness is John the Baptist. "You have sent to John and he has testified to the truth" (**v 33**). Jesus immediately clarifies that his appeal to John as his witness is not because of some "ultimate **epistemological** grounding" (as a modern philosopher would put it) in John as his final authority figure. That is to say, the truth that Jesus is Lord is not ultimately founded or based upon John, or John's witness; for it to be so based upon another, human, witness would effectively de-establish God's ultimate authority. For God to be God, not even

reason or witnesses can be our ultimate authority; God must be our
ultimate authority. So Jesus says, "Not that I accept human testimony;
but I mention it that you may be saved" (**v 34**).

What is so special about the witness of John the Baptist? Partly, it
is because the Jewish leaders themselves had recognized that he was
special: "You have sent to John" (**v 33**). Having recognized him as
an authority figure—someone they need to find out more from and
whose advice they need to ask—they should listen to what he actually
says. But also, John, as Jesus himself tells them, is a special witness:
"John was a lamp that burned and gave light" (**v 35**). This image is
packed with theological truth and evocative power. John was not
merely another rambling preacher; he gave light. He had both content
("gave light") and passion ("burned"). He is a witness that they really
should have listened to.

Second, Jesus' own miracles and signs testify to who he is. Jesus
says, "I have testimony weightier than that of John. For the works that
the Father has given me to finish—the very works that I am doing—
testify that the Father has sent me" (**v 36**). Jesus is saying that the
signs (seven of them in John's Gospel), and ultimately his resurrection
from the dead, are all designed to give them reason to believe that he
is equal with God the Father (20:30-31).

The third witness is the Scriptures. Jesus says that the Bible, and
the word of the Father speaking in the Bible, speak of him (**5:37-44**).
Having established that because he is equal with the Father, to fail to
listen to him is to fail to listen to the Father (**v 37-38**), he now says
they are not listening to him because they do not listen to the word
of the Father as revealed in the Scriptures. "You study the Scriptures
diligently because you think that in them you have eternal life. These
are the very Scriptures that testify about me, yet you refuse to come
to me to have life" (**v 39-40**).

Jesus does not explain here exactly how the Scriptures bear witness about him. Which Scriptures does Jesus have in mind? Are there
particular texts he is thinking about that talk of him? Certainly we can

quote certain passages of the Bible (Isaiah is often in the background to John's Gospel, so Isaiah 53:6 would be an obvious "proof text," one among many possibilities). But Jesus has more in mind here than particular verses or texts. He seems to be saying that all of the Scriptures together are designed to lead the one who searches them to Jesus. The Old Testament inevitably leaves us with certain questions: Who can be righteous? What is the sufficient sacrifice for our sins? Who is the good shepherd in the line of David? Where is this kingdom that was promised? Where is the return from exile that was predicted? All these questions can only find their answer, Jesus is saying, in him and his work, his death, and his resurrection.

But Jesus does explain why it is, at root, that people do not see or understand that the Scriptures speak of him (John **5:41-44**). While Jesus is not primarily concerned with receiving adulation from other people, in the sense that his sense of self-identity and security are not dependent upon what other people think about him (**v 41**), the real problem is that people are unwilling to give him the glory Jesus deserves because they do not even have the love of God within them (**v 42**). When you strip away the intellectualism and the complexity of different approaches to and interpretations of the Scriptures, there

> Our heart attitude allows us to encounter Jesus in the Scriptures, or prevents us from doing so.

is a basic **affectional** orientation, a heart attitude, which either allows us to encounter Jesus in the Scriptures or prevents us from doing so. The question is not: do we read the Scriptures carefully? but rather: do we have the love of God within us?

The truth is that without that love we will see in the Bible what we want to see, and when it says something uncomfortable we will turn down its noise, and drown out its message with other distractions. Bible scholars, teachers, students must have first of all the love of God if they wish to study well. The irony is thick (**v 43**): Jesus is coming in the name of God the Father, but false prophets come to advance their own agenda and "big up" their own selves by the techniques of self-promotion. Yet it is these false prophets, these selfish charlatans, who are more readily received than the one who comes to promote God the Father.

The later history of the Jewish rulers gives sad evidence of the truth of what Jesus is saying: while many of them rejected Jesus as the Christ, they were all too ready to listen to various false prophets and false messiahs, and their willing ear lent to these deceivers led both directly and indirectly to the great catastrophe of the fall of Jerusalem in AD 70. Once again Jesus goes to the very root of the matter in **verse 44**: "How can you believe since you accept glory from one another but do not seek the glory that comes from the only God?" In other words, faith is not simply an intellectual matter. It is a matter of basic commitment and allegiance. If in the end our fundamental desire is to look good to other people, then we will become increasingly blind to, and unable to believe in, the God of the Bible. We do well to ask ourselves regularly: Am I actually seeking glory from God or from other people? Is my blindness to God's ways because of God's silence (surely not: he is a speaking God!) or is it down to my turning a deaf ear to that which draws me to seek glory from God, and turning an itching ear to that which gives me glory from other people?

A Prophet Like Moses

Fourth and finally, Jesus appeals to Moses as a witness. Having mentioned the Scriptures in general, Jesus now appeals to the greatest Old Testament leader of God's people: the prophet Moses. He ends up by again challenging those who are challenging him. Moses "accuses" them to the Father (**v 45**). Why? Partly, because they do not keep the Law of Moses, but also in particular because Moses "wrote about me," Jesus says (**v 46**).

Again, we may ask where precisely Moses writes about Jesus. Clearly he does not do so in a literal, rigid sense. Why then does Jesus imply that it is so obvious that anyone with the right heart, a good will, and a modicum of understanding of what Moses wrote would inevitably believe in Jesus?

> "If their devotion to Moses and his writings was more than lip devotion, they would accept the testimony borne by these writings to the one who was in their midst. But their repudiation of him showed that at heart they repudiated Moses and the prophets. Herein lay their condemnation. For men and women are regularly judged by the light that is available to them."
>
> (Bruce, *The Gospel of John*, page 139)

Jesus seems to believe that the real issue is not intellectual but moral. That is the reason they cannot find Jesus in what Moses wrote, because they are trying to "accept glory from one another" and "do not seek the glory that comes from the only God" (**v 44**).

The obvious place to look for a text linking Moses and the Messiah is Deuteronomy 18:15: "The LORD your God will raise up for you a prophet like me from among you, from your fellow Israelites. You must listen to him." This is, indeed, a link that Jesus' contemporaries would soon start to make (John 6:14).

We should note that claims that Muhammad is the correct fulfillment fall down at the first hurdle. Moses tells us that the prophet that is to come will be Jewish—he will be "from your fellow Israelites." Muhammad was an Arab, and so, apart from any other reason (and there are many), Muhammad fails to be even possibly an option as a fulfillment of the Mosaic promise, if we take the text of Scripture with any seriousness.

So what is it that makes Jesus "like" Moses? Remember, Moses was a redeemer. God used him to rescue his people from Egypt, and then to bring that people to worship God. Jesus too is such a redeemer figure, gathering people to himself through his redemption on the cross.

All that said, it is nevertheless legitimate to ask whether Jesus has this specific text in mind in John 5, or whether he is thinking more generally. If he is thinking more generally, what point is he making? The possibility that Jesus is thinking more generally is raised by his last question in this section, in **verse 47**: "But if you do not believe his writings, how will you believe my words?" (ESV). Note that Jesus talks about Moses' "writings" (plural), and not a specific text in this instance. So most likely, Jesus is viewing "Moses" not as a collection of isolated "texts" but as a person with a particular and distinct message that ran throughout all of what he wrote.

What was that message? Surely it is revealed by the sacrificial system. For some reason people tend to think of Moses as the person of Law, in the sense of moral commandments, and not also as the person who carefully stipulated multiple sacrifices which were intended to point to the one true sacrifice to come. A thinking Jew, observing his own sin, and then pondering the sacrifice of an animal, would ask what was the higher meaning of this sacrifice. A Jew who read the Bible, particularly Isaiah (Isaiah 1 comes to mind, as well as Isaiah 53 again), would inevitably be left with a question about how his sins could be paid for—a question to which only Jesus is the answer. Moses pointed toward the Messiah.

Studying the Scriptures or Meeting With Jesus?

Throughout this section Jesus "peels back the onion" to address not merely "head" issues, but also "heart" ones too. Where do we seek to receive glory from? From God or from people? And how do we read God's word—with pride, seeking to back up our own presuppositions, or with love for God, seeking humbly to hear him? Put another way, do we really encounter Christ as we read the Scriptures?

It is easy to fall into the trap of studying the Scriptures but failing to encounter the Christ behind the Scriptures, the Christ of whom the Scriptures speak, the Word who breathes the word of the Bible. Some conservative churches so excel in the minutiae of understanding the Bible that they fall into the temptation of thinking that it is the minutiae of grammar and text and even the meaning of the text which is saving them. But ultimately, we are in relationship with God, by faith, by believing, and the Scriptures are to lead us to encounter the Christ, meet him, love him, glorify him and find our glory in him. Other churches fail to study the Scriptures at all, or at least do so rarely, thinking that studying the Scripture itself leads to a barren intellectualism. That is a **false dichotomy**: the Scriptures speak of Christ, lead to Christ, and by faith allow us to hear from God himself.

Let us then approach the Bible so that we might have the life "to the full" that is such an integral part of John's agenda in writing this book of his. Let us read the word with love for God, that we might be children of God, born again, renewed in our inmost being by the presence of Jesus, worshiping Jesus in spirit and truth, enjoying and appreciating all these themes that John is developing and weaving together, in such a way that we fall in worship before God, before the Christ, and glory in him.

Questions for reflection

1. "These are the very Scriptures that testify about me." How does or should this truth direct the way you read your Bible?

2. If the Pharisees in this passage were members of your church today, what would they be like?

3. How has this whole chapter given you a greater view and awe of Jesus?

7. FEEDING THE THOUSANDS WITH THE BREAD OF LIFE

This section includes two familiar stories about Jesus. The first is the well-known "sign" of the feeding of the five thousand. The second is the equally well-known miracle of Jesus walking on the water. The questions that we need to answer as we look at these accounts, and indeed their positioning next to each other, are: why is John including them, and why here? They are for a purpose beyond merely a description of the amazing or the fantastical. What is that purpose?

Every time we read John's Gospel, it is important to remind ourselves that John is highly selective in his choice of material. His final verse in the book reminds us that "Jesus did many other things as well" about which we now know nothing (21:25). Why these things? Why are they selected? Why did John put them in this order and at this point in his story, told in precisely this way?

One connection is immediately obvious, and that is the connection between the "bread" with which Jesus feeds the five thousand (**6:5-13**) and Jesus' teaching about himself being the "true bread from heaven" (v 22-59), which we will look at in part two of this chapter. That wider panorama is necessary to keep in view: Jesus performs this miracle of feeding five thousand people to teach us about his true nature and his true identity as the bread from heaven.

Yet, in this first section of chapter 6 that we are looking at now (**v 1-21**), Jesus has not yet uttered his famous words about being the "bread from heaven." We have instead five thousand hungry people, miraculously fed, and then Jesus going for an after-dinner walk on the lake in the middle of a storm. Why? Because Jesus is defining more clearly for those who can see what kind of King he is.

The Packed-Lunch Problem

To begin with, in **verse 1**, we discover that Jesus is on the move again. He is going to the other side of the Sea of Galilee. As he moves, a "great crowd of people" follow him (**v 2**). John immediately explains that Jesus' vast popularity was not because of any sophisticated understanding of theology, much less because the crowd was trying to serve Jesus. No, they were there because Jesus healed "the sick." Jesus was to them a massively effective, utterly inexpensive health-care provider. He was certainly not yet the one that they must serve, much less the one that had a saving agenda for them. Jesus was simply the person who healed the sick. This was his identity in their minds, and it was the reason for Jesus' popularity. There is nothing wrong with looking for health needs to be met by God, nor with finding effective medical provision. But the truth is that Jesus was more than the latest miracle-worker, and much more than merely someone who was concerned only with their physical well-being.

"Then Jesus went up on a mountainside and sat down with his disciples" (**v 3**). This vast crowd was of such a size that Jesus needed to retreat from their pressing concern, gather the core team around him, and consider what to do.

Look at the surprising detail that John now includes to hint that something of significance (a "sign," and not simply a feat of supernatural ability) was about to occur. "The Jewish Passover Festival was near" (**v 4**). Why this detail? Because the Passover was the time above all when the Jews remembered their great prophet Moses, and how through him God had provided them with rescue, leadership, and provision, with **manna** from heaven, even through their wandering years in the desert. It was the season when the thoughts of the Jewish people went especially to the prophet—and perhaps also to the prediction that one day (could it be soon?) there would be another prophet like Moses, who would come as a king to lead God's people into the ultimate promised land. There would have been a spiritual atmosphere around at this moment even among the more earthly-minded of the people of Israel, as is often the case at the great religious feasts, like at Christmas and Easter in Western countries.

Jesus notices that the crowd is not put off by his ascent up a hillside and is still advancing toward him (**v 5**), and so he begins his sign, which will teach them all something of his true identity as the true King. He asks Philip a question: "Where shall we buy bread for these people to eat?" (**v 5**). We are told this is to "test him" (**v 6**)—not in the sense of an unfair examination, but in the sense of giving Philip a challenge to see if he can rise to it and begin to sense who Jesus truly is. Philip has no idea where to buy bread, and immediately thinks of the vast amount of money it would require: "more than half a year's wages" (**v 7**). In America, the national average wage index was $44,888.16 in 2013. Philip is saying, roughly speaking, that to give all these people bread would cost over $20,000. Unsurprisingly, he is not carrying that amount of cash with him!

Andrew is also scratching his head, wondering what on earth to do about the problem they now find themselves facing. Everyone knows that crowds can quickly turn nasty if things go wrong, and to find a crowd of several thousand people growing increasingly hungry was not a pleasant thought for anyone. Andrew then, almost half-jokingly, points out that there is a boy nearby who has a small picnic with him (**v 8-9**). You can imagine them chatting together:

Jesus: *Where will we feed all this lot?*

Philip: *No idea—I'm not carrying tens of thousands of dollars in my back pocket.*

Andrew: *The good news is that over there that boy has a small picnic.*

But then Jesus takes charge. As ever, Jesus is using the events around him, shaping them, to show those who will see what his true agenda is and, here, who he truly is. He says, "Have the people sit down" (**v 10**). There were five thousand men there, and they sat down; there was plenty of room for them all to find a place to sit. The crowd itself was almost certainly larger than five thousand: five thousand men not counting the women and children, some of whom were presumably also present, but were not counted in a typical head count of the day as this was done by heads of family units. (We know there was at least one boy there!)

In perhaps the greatest understatement ever written, in **verse 11** John describes Jesus' technique. He took the loaves from the boy (was he hesitant to give up his picnic, I wonder?), simply "gave thanks," and then the food was "distributed" to those who were seated. This was no magic trick; this was no occult power. Jesus offered a prayer of thanks, and the food was miraculously multiplied. Simple—for Jesus, that is.

And there was more to come. The people "all had enough to eat" (**v 12**). That is, they had more than enough and were full to bursting. Jesus told the disciples to gather up what was left, and when they did so, they discovered that not only did Jesus provide enough, but he provided more than enough; they filled "twelve baskets with the pieces of the five barley loaves left over" (**v 13**).

Jesus is making a point. He is showing them that he is Someone extraordinary. He is the kind of person who does a miracle, and does it not with great effort and achieving just enough—he does it exuberantly, abundantly, and to overflowing. Five thousand men to feed? A small picnic with which to feed them? No problem—and you can have twelve baskets of leftover food as well.

"The feeding sign in John 6 goes beyond mere repetition of the miracles performed by Moses. It seems to signal a whole new Exodus, far greater than that celebrated at the Passover. God acts to give Israel true bread from heaven as opposed to the manna, which was much less than [true, real, genuine] in comparison with Jesus."

(Hamid-Khani, *Revelation and Concealment of Christ*, page 263)

The people realize that something astonishing has happened (**v 14**)—who could not? They "saw the sign," and they make the right conclusion, though in the wrong way. Accurately, they realize that "surely this is the Prophet who is to come into the world." Jesus is the Prophet that Moses had predicted would come, though he is far more than merely another prophet. They are half right in their understanding of Jesus. But they are also wrong in how they perceive this prophet should act, and what that will mean for them. Like crowds the world over, once you get them moving, they tend to keep on moving in the same direction; subtlety, nuance, discretion and balance are not easy for a massed crowd to display. Jesus realizes that they have gone from viewing him as an all-in-one free healthcare solution to an aggressive military ruler about to throw out the Romans and reestablish the **Davidic kingdom**—from one extreme to another (**v 15**). Seeing they are about to "come and make him king by force," he withdraws again to the mountain. Further up, and further in, away from the madding crowd.

> The people make the right conclusion, in the wrong way.

What kind of King is this? He is not merely a miracle worker. He is not merely a prophet. He is not merely a king trying to gain his throne by a popular uprising. Jesus is Something Else and is Someone Else. But who?

The Man on the Water

Now the most amazing part of this two-part story begins. The disciples, perhaps now having no idea where Jesus has gone, start once more across the Sea of Galilee (**v 16-17**). On occasion you get the impression that Jesus would, to the disciples, have seemed a bit like Gandalf in *The Hobbit*—always appearing and then suddenly disappearing again. Where is he off to now? The disciples decided to go back to where they had come from to see if they could find him. A storm began, or at least a "strong wind" (**v 18**). They were now "about three or four miles" from the shore (**v 19**), a long way from any possible tricks with sandbars and the like, and there was a strong wind blowing—so no one could be fooled into thinking that what was about to happen was normal or natural.

Suddenly, "they saw Jesus approaching the boat, walking on the water; and they were frightened" (**v 19**). What is most amazing about this description is that now their fears were beginning to be rightly placed. They were not frightened of the strong winds; they were frightened of Jesus. We can imagine the scene as calmly, without haste or worry, with commensurate ease and careful solemnity, with grace of manner and deliberate pace, those unhurrying feet walk steadily—in the midst of strong winds, miles out from the shore—on the water. It would scare you half out of your mind if you saw it.

But Jesus says that those who do see it are not to be afraid. Yes, they are beginning to see that this is Someone Else. And yet this Someone Else is on their side. He is for them, not against them: "It is I; don't be afraid" (**v 20**).

Who is this? "It is I" seems designed to resemble the Hebrew phrase "I AM," the personal name of God by which he revealed himself to Moses and his people in Exodus 3:13-14. *I AM*, Jesus says; and he was, and he is, and he is today. Yesterday, today, and forever: *I AM, Yahweh, Jehovah, the LORD, Jesus*.

Most likely, all this significance was not present in the minds of the disciples as they heard Jesus speak. His choice of words was also a way of saying "It is me" more normally. But for John to choose this expression, to select it for us, is to prepare us (as the disciples were being prepared) to hear again from Jesus' lips the great claim of John 8:58: "'Very truly I tell you,' Jesus answered, 'before Abraham was born, I am!'" He was I AM before Abraham's day, and he was I AM in John's day, and he still is I AM today.

"Then they were willing to take him into the boat" (**6:21**). Had they left him standing to the side while they huddled together, before he spoke? Now they received him gladly, and in a final miracle, Jesus' presence in their boat meant that now—"immediately"—the boat landed on the other side.

What kind of King is this? That is the question that faces us at the end of this part of the story. He is far greater than we can imagine, and his claim upon our lives is more significant than our tendency to domesticate God so often allows. He is King of kings and Lord of lords, the kind of King who can calm a storm and do so imme-diately—the great I AM. Is this how we treat Jesus? Do we worship him? Do we allow the "storms" in our lives to triumph over the scale of the majesty of this Jesus? Or are the situations of our personal daily struggles and the mammoth complexities of our world brought to heel, and brought into perspective, by the astonishing power of this King Jesus?

Questions for reflection

1. "Jesus realizes that they have gone from viewing him as an all-in-one free healthcare solution to an aggressive military ruler." What do these two misunderstandings of the nature of Jesus' kingship look like in your society or church?

2. How you ever felt such awe for Jesus that you've needed to hear his reassurance that you don't need to be afraid of him? If not, might it be that your view of Jesus is simply too small?

3. What looms larger for you today—the storms of your life, or the power of King Jesus? What difference will his power make to the way you view your day?

PART TWO

We come now to one of the more lengthy discourses in the Gospel of John (and so this second part of this chapter is one of the lengthier parts in this book on the Gospel of John!). Contained in it are various puzzles of some complexity, but basically the whole discussion is framed by Jesus' just-completed feeding of the five thousand. This marks Jesus out as a prophet at least on equal terms with Moses, through whom God provided manna to his people in Israel; but Jesus wants to take the discussion several steps further. He is not just offering "bread"; he is offering "the bread of life." What does that mean?

More Than a Good Meal

First, in **verses 22-24**, we see how Jesus' miracle had produced a frantic interest on the part of many—they were "in search of Jesus." They could not figure out where he had gone, and when they finally discovered him, they couldn't see how he had arrived there, not having witnessed the perhaps still more remarkable miracle of Jesus' walking on the water in verses 16-21.

Eventually, they find Jesus (**v 25**). Their immediate question is understandable: "Rabbi, when did you get here?" or, in effect, *How on earth did you get here?* Jesus does not answer by going into details about his ability to stroll across the lake unassisted by a boat, but instead addresses their spiritual emptiness head on. "Very truly I tell you [one of Jesus' characteristic ways of emphasizing the significance of what is about to follow], you are looking for me, not because you saw the signs I performed but because you ate the loaves and had your fill" (**v 26**).

Jesus is saying that their spiritual condition is not just relatively superficial (they saw signs and therefore are seeking after the miracle-worker); it is worse than that, for what look like spiritual desires are really only basic material desires. They have had a good meal, and they want to keep on being fed! And so Jesus redirects their desires by telling them that, generally speaking, they are not to "work for food that spoils, but for food that endures to eternal life" (**v 27**). Jesus does not mean that it is wrong to earn a living—the Bible is very clear elsewhere that we must work in order to eat (2 Thessalonians 3:10, 12). Jesus does mean that they should not work merely for food; that is, they should not be fixated on material well-being. It is necessary to take care of the body and to work for food and material survival. But this should not be the focus of our lives. Humans were made for more than the material. Jesus is calling them to a higher and more important "work." He wants them to work "for food that endures to eternal life, which the Son of Man will give you. For on him God the Father has placed his seal of approval" (John **6:27**).

It is important to realize that though Jesus is asking them to "work," he is not thereby suggesting that they will "earn" this eternal life. No, it is still a gift, and a gift that must be given only by Jesus, because only on him has the Father "placed his seal of approval." That is, Jesus is God's appointed Savior, and it is he who must give us this eternal life. Jesus is not making a **works-righteousness** point; he is just saying that the fundamental concern of our lives should not merely be about doing well materially. The fundamental concern of our lives should be about eternal life, and that is in his gift alone.

Never Hunger Again

Verse 28 is the follow-up question from those who have followed him across the lake. It suggests that they have missed most, if not all, of the subtlety of Jesus' reply. So Jesus makes it plain in a statement that is one of the greatest evangelistic texts of all time: "The work of God is this: to believe in the one he has sent" (**v 29**).

Jesus wants them to believe in him in some exclusive and utterly committed fashion. So they ask in return why they should so believe in him. Or to put it more exactly, they ask what sort of sign he will give them (**v 30**). **Verses 30-31** must contain one of the most idiotic statements ever uttered. Remember, these are the people who have just seen the feeding of the five thousand, and they would like to be able to have some more bread for free. But now they ask Jesus whether he will give them bread from heaven, as Moses did. Surely Jesus must have been tempted to reply, *What do you think I just did?!*

Instead, he is utterly gracious and uses their slow pace of processing to utter another "Very truly I tell you" statement packed with meaning: "It is not Moses who has given you the bread from heaven" (**v 32**). They knew that, but perhaps it was good for them to be reminded that Moses was merely a channel, not the author, of the miracle of the manna itself. No, the manna-bread came from the Father in heaven. And now in Jesus' day, the bread of God is actually not just the feeding of the 5,000 but what that feeding represents—namely Jesus himself, he who "comes down from heaven and gives life to the world" (**v 33**).

Now we come to it. They want this bread (**v 34**). Where is it? "I am the bread of life. Whoever comes to me will never go hungry, and whoever believes in me will never be thirsty" (**v 35**). What a glorious promise! What sweet truth! Relish and enjoy him, as your Lord; "come to [him]," and you will never thirst, never hunger, always be fully and eternally satisfied.

This must have appeared to be an astonishing claim, and more than a little enigmatic when first uttered (and perhaps it still seems so today). Clearly Jesus was not speaking in a directly literal way. You can only eat bread; you can't also drink it. We come to Jesus as the "bread of life," and in so coming to him we find that both our need for food is satisfied (we will never go "hungry"), and also our need for drink is satisfied (we will never go "thirsty"). If Jesus meant "bread of life" literally here, he could not have encouraged them to come and not be thirsty. It is a metaphor—picture-language—describing something beyond the mundanely literal. But what does the metaphor mean?

The next few verses, perhaps somewhat frustratingly to them (and very possibly to us), do not really explain what Jesus means by being the bread of life. Instead they explain the consequences of the fact that Jesus is the bread of life. **Verse 36** tells us that some do not believe even though they have seen him. **Verse 37** is a promise precious to every Christian: learn it, consume it, and delight in it. Whoever comes to Jesus he will never drive away. Why is that? Because that is the will of God himself. It is clear from chapter 1 and elsewhere that Jesus is fully God. In the mystery of the Trinity, the will of the Father God, with which the Son completely and utterly concurs, is specifically that none should be snatched from Jesus. This explanation of the **perseverance** of true Christians—that it is because of the will of the Father God—should release and protect us from the suspicion that somehow God the Father is sterner and Jesus the Son is kinder. On the contrary: their will is the same on this as on every other matter:

> "Let it suffice that the gospel will always have the power to gather the **elect** to salvation."
>
> (Calvin, *Calvin's New Testament Commentaries,* Vol. 1, page 161)

Saved or Grumbling

How would the crowd react? They grumbled (**v 41**). What offended them was that Jesus was, they thought, merely human; or rather, they knew he was human and so they assumed that he was merely human. He was Joseph's son, they thought, and therefore Jesus could not in any sense be "from heaven" (**v 42**).

Jesus rebukes them in **verse 43**: "Stop grumbling among yourselves." Why? Because "no one can come to me unless the Father who sent me draws them" (**v 44**). In other words, grumbling is a dangerous thing to do. It still is today. For instance, when we "grumble" that Jesus has no right to call us to a dangerous task, or to call us to serve without recognition in the background, or to exercise his right of lordship over our lives, we place ourselves in opposition to his good rule. A simple grumble can have dangerous effects—as Israel well knew, and about which we are well instructed (1 Corinthians 10:10). Don't think that your discussion among yourselves will determine who

Jesus is and whether he can save you; the Father will save whom he wills, and grumbling against Jesus may only prove to show that you are not among that number.

John **6:44** should not be taken in a **fatalistic** sense. On one hand, it is impossible to believe in Jesus unless God the Father.draws us. On the other hand, Jesus is making it very clear over and over again that we are to believe in him. If we believe in Jesus, it is a sign that God the Father has drawn us; so believe in Jesus and be assured that God has drawn you to him! **Election** is intended to encourage Christians that they are secure; it is never or very rarely preached to non-Christians, for whom the message is instead, "Believe and you will be saved." The nineteenth-century evangelist D.L. Moody gave an old illustration that is still helpful. When you are saved, it's as if you walk through a door with a sign over it saying, "Come to me all you who are weary and heavy laden and I will give you rest." You walk through the door and when you look back, you see on the other side of the door the words, "Before the creation of the world I knew you." Believe, and you will be saved; and if you are saved, you are secure, for God the Father has drawn you. This is a warning against grumbling; instead, be humble because even our coming to Jesus is ultimately in God's hands, and not ours.

Jesus assumes a close relationship between divine sovereignty and human responsibility, as Köstenberger outlines:

"John **6:44-46** points to the cooperative effort between the Father and the Son in bringing a person to salvation. While salvation is the result of the Father's drawing work, it is brought about by an individual's believing reception of God's revelation in Jesus." (*John*, page 214)

Jesus "will raise them up at the last day" (**v 44**). There is a resurrection to come for those who believe in Jesus. Now Jesus begins to address the specifics of their grumbling.

How is it that he could be who he says he is? Because Jesus is fulfilling the promise that they would all be "taught by God" (**v 45**). In other words, his direct, personal, present, human teaching of them is the fulfillment of God's promise of direct, personal, divine teaching of them as prophesied in the Old Testament (Isaiah 54:13). This all builds to another great proclamation of the identity of Jesus (John **6:46**), and its **corollary** that if we believe in Jesus we have eternal life (**v 47**). What greater claim could there be?! What greater promise could there be?! We "have" eternal life; when we believe, we switch from the realm of death to the realm of life, and not even our physical death can interrupt that new reality which is ours through faith in this Jesus.

Then Jesus continues to expand on this point, repeating again, "I am the bread of life" (**v 48**), urging them to believe in him and so receive eternal life, and to believe that this life is the gift of the Father, and so they can only come to him if the Father draws them. He is greater even than that miraculous gift of manna, for that did not give them eternal life (**v 49**), but this—this Jesus—is now the bread from heaven, so that if someone eats of him—trusts in him—they will never die eternally (**v 50**).

And then… Jesus concludes this section with a yet more astonishing statement at the end of **verse 51**: "This bread is my flesh, which I will give for the life of the world."

Convoluted and Controversial

This verse and the section that follows it have a highly convoluted and controversial history in the Christian church. Essentially, those from very **high-church** and Roman Catholic traditions believe that Jesus was talking about the Lord's Supper or Eucharist. You can see why, as the crowd ask again (**v 52**) what on earth Jesus can mean by this astonishing statement. Jesus replies in yet more extraordinary ways (**v 53**). "Whoever eats my flesh and drinks my blood has eternal life, and I will raise them up at the last day" (**v 54**). He even says, "For my flesh is real food and my blood is real drink" (**v 55**). He suggests that this is key to his presence with them and being for them—in a sense "in" them spiritually: "Whoever eats my flesh and drinks my blood remains in me, and I in them" (**v 56**). His unique spiritual connection to the Father means that whoever "feeds" on him will "live" (**v 57**). This is the bread that came down from heaven, and is not like the manna that their forefathers ate, for whoever "feeds" on this "bread" will live forever (**v 58**). This teaching took place at Capernaum in the synagogue (**v 59**).

What does Jesus mean? Some options must be immediately ruled out. Jesus cannot mean that they should literally eat him and drink his blood. No one then or since has thought that Jesus is commending cannibalism. If that is not the case, then Jesus must be intending some sort of metaphorical language, and the only question is: what is the metaphor pointing to? Could Jesus mean the ceremony that Christians call "the Lord's Supper"? After all, at that point bread and drink are consumed, and does not Jesus say that his flesh is "real food" and his blood is "real drink"?

However, there are several reasons for insisting that Jesus could not mean the Lord's Supper. For one, and most obviously, Jesus has not yet instituted the Lord's Supper. It does not necessarily follow that he could not mean it (after all, he does talk prophetically about things that have not occurred), but it makes it unlikely. How could Jesus expect a complicated metaphor to be understood to refer to something which his original hearers did not even know would exist at the time that they heard him teaching (and which did not even feature later in John's Gospel)? It begins to strain credibility.

> This reality is a shadowland, and we will only experience the real world in the new earth.

Additionally, given that Jesus must be using some metaphor here, the idea that he must be talking about the Lord's Supper on the basis that it would be the least metaphorical option begins to look thin. After all, even those Roman Catholics who believe that the "host" literally is Jesus think that that bread is Jesus in a *different* manner than Jesus was at the time he stood on earth and spoke here in John 6. Again, the key phrase is in **verse 55**: "real food" and "real drink" need not imply that Jesus means literal edibles. Jesus could be using "real" to mean that the drink and food are symbolic representations of a higher truth: in many ways this world, this life, this reality is a "shadowland," and we will only experience the real world in the new heaven and the new earth. This reality, this "truth" (ESV), could be that of the "grace and truth" that Jesus brought with him as he preached the gospel (1:17).

If, though, Jesus does not mean something literal or sacramental by these words, then what does he mean? Jesus himself explains when the disciples start to question him: "This is a hard teaching. Who can accept it?" (**6:60**). The teaching is hard to understand, hard to listen to, and hard therefore to accept and follow in practice. Now the disciples are "grumbling" too (**v 61**). But they are confused, not because they are thinking insufficiently literally but because they are thinking insufficiently spiritually. If they could not swallow the teaching he had just given them, how would they cope if they were to "see the Son of Man ascend to where he was before" (**v 62**)? They need to open their minds to a deeper and more spiritual reality than physical bread.

So Jesus makes it absolutely crystal clear in **verse 63**: "The Spirit gives life; the flesh counts for nothing. The words I have spoken to you—they are full of the Spirit and life." That is, Jesus does not mean literal food of any kind ("real" does not always equal "literal"); he means something spiritual (as one of Jesus' disciples is about to grasp, in **verses 68-69**). Indeed, the "flesh" (which is material) counts for nothing. If we just think in physical and material terms, we will not understand what Jesus is saying.

Some would not understand this because they would not "believe," and there was even one who would betray him (**v 64**). Unless the Father enables us, we cannot come to the Son (**v 65**). This follow-up explanation turns even some of Jesus' disciples away from him (**v 66**). It is a "hard teaching."

Where Else Would We Go?

Now Jesus turns to the Twelve: "You do not want to leave too, do you?" (**v 67**). On this occasion, Peter gives a pitch perfect answer— one which summarizes the meaning of the whole "bread of life" discourse and which expresses the heartfelt belief of the follower of Jesus: "Lord, to whom shall we go? You have the words of eternal life. We have come to believe and to know that you are the Holy One of God" (**v 68-69**).

Jesus is talking about believing in him as God's Savior, the one in whom are the words of eternal life. We eat of his flesh and we drink of his blood by believing in him, as Peter explains. There is no other food we can find that will sustain us for eternity. Every believer has come to the point of saying, "However hard this may get, I have nowhere else to go, because only here do I find life for eternity."

And not everyone gets that. Even among the Twelve there was one who did not get it: Judas. **Verses 70-71** end this discourse on a som- ber and yet realistic note. They also underline the main point of the whole section again: Jesus wants us to believe in him, to receive life eternal, and for that to happen the Father must choose us. Even one of his closest disciples did not believe. Do you?

Questions for reflection

1. "'Come to [him],' and you will never thirst, never hunger, always be fully and eternally satisfied." When this week will you most need to remember this?

2. How does enjoying a secure salvation undermine the need for, and any excuse for, grumbling?

3. How does Jesus' teaching here cause you to love him more?

8. RIVERS FLOW AND STONES LIE STILL

In the Nevada Desert in America each summer, there is a festival—the "Burning Man" festival. In 2015, 70,000 people attended. Beginning as a spontaneous act of self-expression, this burning of a human effigy at the summer solstice has developed into a large-scale festival. Such gatherings have always made waves, in the past as now. Well, this section of John's Gospel is a long one to look at in one sitting, but it is important to see how it all fits together—even if subsequently you go back and examine in more detail all the constituent parts. What ties it all together is that it all takes place during a festival—the Festival of Tabernacles (**7:2**).

The Festival of Tabernacles was one of the great annual feasts given by God to his people in the Old Testament. Moses commanded God's people that they should "live in temporary shelters for seven days" (Leviticus 23:42), because in so doing they were reminding themselves of God's rescue of them from Egypt: "So your descendants will know that I had the Israelites live in temporary shelters when I brought them out of Egypt" (Leviticus 23:43).

Additionally, it is probable—and this is a key detail in order to explain the central event of John 7—that there was an especial emphasis upon water. A water libation—that is, a pouring out of water—was performed at the temple, perhaps after the high priest had led a procession from the Pool of Siloam back to the temple. As the water was poured out, it is likely they would have recited Psalm 118, regarded as a messianic psalm: "LORD, save us! LORD, grant us success! Blessed is he who comes in the name of the LORD. From the house of the LORD we bless you" (Psalm 118:25-26).

Once we grasp this basic overall context of the Festival of Tabernacles, in particular the water ceremony, John **7:37-38** begins to become exciting. It is, I think, one of the most powerful moments in the whole Gospel. Imagine the scene with masses of people, water libations taking place in the background, and Psalm 118 being recited, and Jesus then standing and declaring, "Let anyone who is thirsty come to me and drink. Whoever believes in me, as Scripture has said, rivers of living water will flow from within them." All that begins to set the trajectory for this great event in John 7. Let us first, though, walk through the passage bit by bit.

Will He Stay or Will He Go?

In John **7:1**, we are reminded that the stakes are being raised. The Jewish leaders are not only set against Jesus; they are even seeking to kill him. At this point it's important to underline that when John says "the Jews" (ESV), he does not mean in any way to imply an antisemitic message. After all, he himself was a Jew, as was Jesus. No, John seems often to use the word "Jew" in these contexts as a kind of shorthand for "the Jewish rulers who were against Jesus." At any rate, they were against Jesus.

Yet still Jesus' brothers try to persuade him to go the festival (**v 3**). Their reason for doing so is entirely misconceived. They perceive that Jesus is a "mover and shaker." He clearly has the "personality" to become well known. Does he want that or not? If he wants that, he should stop being so bashful and hiding away, and instead go up to the great festival to make a name for himself (**v 3-4**). Perhaps they are seeking to call his bluff, since they do not believe his claims about himself (**v 5**).

Interestingly, Jesus does not entirely dismiss their idea. It is simply that his "time is not yet here" (**v 6**). There will be a moment when he receives due attention, but his "time" will be the time of his cross and resurrection. It is right for Jesus to be acclaimed, but their understanding of Jesus' path to glory is very different from the path to the cross that he must tread. The commentator Leon Morris puts it like this:

"John is clear that others do not lay down the pattern for Jesus. He is supremely the master of every situation. So in this case he went up when he was ready and in the way he chose."

(The Gospel according to John, page 355)

And so Jesus tells his brothers that there will be opposition to him (**v 7**), as they already know, but also that the time will come when they will see even more opposition—even his crucifixion; and so Jesus tells them to go on ahead to the feast (**v 8**). It is probable that in some manuscripts a somewhat overzealous copyist inserted the addition of "yet" here (indicated in the footnote) because he could not quite understand why Jesus said, "I am not going up to this festival" when the rest of the story shows that he did go. But such an insertion is unnecessary: Jesus meant that he was not going up to the festival at the same time as they were going, for his time had not "yet" fully come.

The Center of Attention

So Jesus for the time being remains in Galilee (**v 9**), but then goes up to Jerusalem in secret at first (**v 10**). He discovers that everyone is muttering about him. Clearly he is the talk of the festival. Some are for him; others are against—and the Jewish leaders are hoping to find him (**v 11-12**). No one will openly speak of him because they are afraid of the Jewish leaders (**v 13**).

Now about halfway through the seven-day festival, Jesus begins to teach (**v 14**). What is marvelous about his teaching is that Jesus does not seem to have the right kind of credentials or background to teach with such authority (**v 15**). He has not been to their rabbinic schools, and yet he knows what he is talking about. Jesus tries to point them to the significance of what they have pointed out: "My teaching is not my own. It comes from the one who sent me" (**v 16**).

Verse 17 has puzzled some Christians. But it probably merely means that if someone really wants to know whether Jesus is who he says he is (that is, it's their "will" to do "God's will"), then the evidence is sufficient to find out. What they will discover is that Jesus is not speaking "on [his] own" authority (or "from himself," **v 18**) and is not seeking his own glory; he is not self-serving or selfish in his claim to be someone worth listening to and following. Rather, he is seeking the glory of God, and therefore his claim is true and is not deceptive. The explanation is couched in a principle: namely, that if someone is out for their own good and their own glory, they are not someone worth following, but if they are looking out for God's glory, then they can be trusted.

Next Jesus begins to expose his opponents' hypocrisy, showing that they are not doing "the will of God," and therefore they find it hard to believe that he is who he says he is. They are questioning his teaching (**v 17**), but they have Moses' teaching, which they claim to accept (**v 19**), and yet they are not really following Moses' law; instead they are doing the very opposite of what Moses would do. They are really trying to kill him, he tells them. They deny it, yet, as the saying goes, "they protesteth too much"; they say he is demonic to suggest they are trying to kill him (**v 20**), even as the knife rests in their hands.

Jesus points out the original cause of their offense—"I did one miracle" (**v 21**), referring all the way back to his healing of a man on a Sabbath (5:1-16). This had clearly stuck in their throats. As far as the Jews were concerned, it was the beginning of the end for this charismatic young preacher. Jesus points out how illogical they are being: they circumcise on a Sabbath, so why should he not heal on a Sabbath (**7:22-23**)? "Stop judging by mere appearances, but instead judge correctly" (**v 24**). *Think!* says Jesus. *Go beyond the merely external and formal, and discern the work of God.*

Is This the Messiah?

Next, in **verse 25**, a different group chimes in—not the rulers but likely the wider crowd. They wonder whether indeed the Jewish rulers are trying to kill this man. They conclude that, since Jesus is not being killed even though he is speaking publicly, the rulers must have decided that he is the Messiah or Christ (**v 26**). This is certainly a false conclusion, but you can see how a crowd might begin to wonder. Jesus is, as it were, sitting in the director's chair, having previously been charged with high treason, so presumably the rulers have decided he did nothing wrong and is in fact the divine person he has claimed to be.

Having, it appears, started out in a promising direction, nonetheless this wider group finally decides that if the rulers think Jesus is the Messiah, they must be wrong! This is because these people "know where this man is from" (**v 27**). He doesn't fulfill the credentials of their tightly configured messianic resumé. In response, Jesus raises the stakes (**v 28-29**). He comes not from Nazareth but from God.

This, of course, is deeply shocking and so they "tried to seize him," but they do not actually manage it because "his hour had not yet come" (**v 30**). We are told nothing more beyond that. God is sovereignly in control, Jesus is in charge, and his death will be at the moment of his decision. Not yet.

Now a further group comes into view. "Many in the crowd believed in him" (**v 31**). They ask the right question, as the less learned and the more humble do so often: "When the Messiah comes, will he perform more signs than this man?"

The Pharisees are incensed by the possibility that people are "whispering" that Jesus indeed is the Christ, so they decide, as it were, to act on their arrest warrant and actually send the temple officers to arrest him (**v 32**), presumably for disturbing the peace as

> These officers come to arrest Jesus, and he gives them a Bible study!

well as for his outrageous claim to be the Messiah. Jesus, exerting his royal authority, proceeds to give these arresting officers a rather straightforward theology lesson. They come to arrest him, and he gives them a Bible study! "I am with you for only a short time, and then I am going to the one who sent me. You will look for me, but you will not find me; and where I am, you cannot come" (**v 33-34**). This completely nonplusses them (**v 35-36**), and while they are trying to figure out the riddle, Jesus quietly slips away. Jesus is talking of his death, resurrection, and ascension—but of course they have no idea, for it is not yet his time. And Jesus moves on.

Rivers of Living Water

And so we come to the key moment. John signals its importance with bright rhetorical lights: "On the last and greatest day of the festival, Jesus stood and said in a loud voice…" (**v 37**). This is as good as saying, "Reader, this is the point… the big moment's about to come… cue fanfare, pause, ready… here we go." And so Jesus says, "Let anyone who is thirsty come to me and drink. Whoever believes in me, as Scripture has said, rivers of living water will flow from within them" (**v 37-38**).

Remember all the water in the background, all the libations being poured out; and Jesus says that he is the water of life. He is the one in whom they need to believe. If they do, then springs of living water, water of life, will flow out of the heart. To which Scripture is Jesus referring? Many possibilities could be given, and it may be that Jesus is summarizing a whole thread through the Scriptures, rather than quoting a particular verse. To my mind, though, Isaiah 55:1a best sums up the spirit of what Jesus is fulfilling: "Come, all you who are thirsty, come to the waters." As Spurgeon put it:

> "To the unbeliever, Christ is nothing. But to the Believer, Christ is everything. To the unbeliever, a mere opinion about Christ is everything. To the true Believer, the saving knowledge of Christ has covered up all mere opinions concerning Him. He knows Christ, and lives in him, and Christ also lives in him."
>
> (Sermon #2710, Volume 47)

In John **7:39**, John immediately tells us what Jesus means. He is referring to the gift of the Holy Spirit. The Spirit who dwells within all true

Christians, connected to us inescapably by divine cords that cannot be broken, gives us a spring of living water that wells up within. This is what happens to all who truly believe in Jesus. This life, this spiritual life, this eternal life satisfying, quenching every desire and longing of the human breast—drink, reader, drink.

At this, some begin to believe—at least after a fashion. Some think he is the One, and some do not (**v 40-42**); "the people were divided" (**v 43**). Ironically, they rightly think that the Messiah will be of the line of David and from Bethlehem, but they are so astonishingly ignorant as not to realize that this promise is fulfilled in Jesus! In John's inspired narrative genius, he uses this irony to underline their opposition. Everyone knew Jesus was descended from David and from Bethlehem, apart from them! It is often the case that ignorance is the mother of prejudice, and prejudice is fathered by antipathy to the person concerned. They could have found out the truth, but they did not. Once more some see the best solution is to arrest him; others are not so sure. Again, nothing happens (**v 44**).

The Pharisees are confused and upset about this (**v 45**). They have sent officers to arrest Jesus. Instead of doing that, they just return empty-handed, for "no one ever spoke the way this man does" (**v 46**). There are many proofs of Jesus' divinity that may be given, but one of the most overlooked (though at the same time most impressive to those who first came across Jesus) was the sheer power and authority of his spoken words. No one ever spoke like this man—because he was not a mere man.

The strain on the Pharisees is starting to show now (**v 47-48**), and they start to curse the people that they are sworn to protect (**v 49**). Beware when religious leaders start to shun the people they are meant to serve. But the Pharisees themselves are no longer completely united. Nicodemus, one of the ruling body, who in John 3 had secretly gone to see Jesus at night (**v 50**), asks them a pointed question (**v 51**): "Does our law condemn a man without first hearing him to find out what he has been doing?" It is the kind of question that is asked in a court of law.

Nicodemus' objection only serves to underline that things are looking bad for Jesus. His one friend is shouted down: "A prophet does not come out of Galilee" (**v 52**). Yet Jesus is from God, as he has taught.

The Pharisees are hardening even as they are cracking; but we should be drinking. "Let anyone who is thirsty come to me and drink. Whoever believes in me, as Scripture has said, rivers of living water will flow from within them" (**v 37-38**). When we come to Jesus in faith, when we, through trusting in him, "drink" from him, out of our hearts will flow rivers of living water. Do you treat Jesus as the great thirst-quencher? When you are tired, or frustrated, or needing renewal, do you go to other promisers of satisfaction—to entertainment or comfort of one kind or another? Or do you see in Jesus, and find in Jesus, the great soul-satisfaction that he here guarantees for those who follow him?

Questions for reflection

1. An old proverb says, "There's none so blind as those that will not see." How can we prevent over-familiarity with the Bible from seeing the truth right in front of us?

2. What do you think it means to experience the Spirit's streams of living water flowing within you?

3. Confusion over who Jesus is will often be claimed as evidence that he cannot be God, or at least not the only true God. How does this passage suggest that human confusion over his identity is actually an indication of the truth of his divine claims?

PART TWO

Sexual immorality is as old as the hills; but its preponderance in modern societies seems to be increasing and not abating. At the same time, as so often, religiosity can position itself in a judgmental and angular way towards our sins, rather than in a saving and transforming way to generate holiness and gospel light.

This section of John brings Jesus face to face with sexual immorality. But this section includes a segment that has long been doubted as to the correctness of its textual location in this part of John's Gospel. This is not the place to rehearse the arguments about the textual **veracity** or otherwise of the story of the woman caught in adultery. Suffice it to say that if this account is not originally a part of this narrative, it certainly fits well, and seems to me to have definitely been authentic to Christ, whether or not it was originally located here or elsewhere in the Gospels. The judgment of the woman, Jesus' compassion and salvation, and the judgmental pharisaical approach are themes that we meet elsewhere in John's Gospel, and they are masterfully interwoven here to reveal Jesus as the great hope ("the light"), which we all need to light up our darkness.

The Woman Caught in Adultery

The first section of this narrative deals with a particular matter of sexual adultery. Jesus had gone up to the nearby Mount of Olives (**8:1**), close to the ancient city of Jerusalem. Early the next morning he returns to the temple (**v 2**), and the action begins. Jesus is magnetic: "all the people gathered around him." Do we crowd the rooms where the Bible is taught?

The teachers of the law and the Pharisees come to him too (**v 3**), but with a different intention. Clearly, this is a set-up. They have "brought in a woman caught in adultery," perhaps suggesting she had been caught red-handed, but also possibly that the evidence for her adultery was so overwhelming as to be beyond doubt (**v 3-4**). It is interesting that the man is absent. It does take two to tango, and the man is equally guilty of adultery—and yet he is not here. The scribes and Pharisees are immediately displaying a **chauvinistic** manipulation of the Old Testament text, since that text determines that both parties are equally guilty (Leviticus 20:10). Not for them, though: the woman, specifically, is brought forward for justice, while the man is nowhere to be seen.

Now comes the question—again an attempt to put Jesus to the test by seeing whether he will agree with Moses. "In the Law Moses commanded us to stone such women. Now what do you say?" (John **8:5**). It was indeed true that the penalty for adultery, according to the Law of Moses in Leviticus 20:10, was death. But again, it was for both the man and woman. And, within the context of the law as a whole, replete with sacrifices for those guilty of sin, there was remedy for sin within the mercy of God for the repentant sinner. If, according to the law, the adulterer was always to be put to death, whatever the repentant nature of his heart, then Psalm 51 would never have been written, and David (who was both an adulterer and a murderer— 2 Samuel 11) would never have been able to be forgiven.

But justice, far less mercy, is not what the scribes and Pharisees are after. They want to trap Jesus so that they can accuse him (John **8:6**). Is there a **salacious** attraction to scandal present in this whole event too? A moistening of the lips—a subtle but nonetheless real delight in the poor woman's plight?

Presumably Jesus, known as a man of mercy, would be expected to want to have mercy on this poor woman, but with his opponents having now quoted the authority of Moses, if he does seek to rescue the woman, he will be in trouble. On the other hand, if he does not—if he agrees to their accusation—much of Jesus' reputation and popularity might begin to slip away. And far more seriously, this woman will die. Their quoting Scripture in defense of a deeply un-popular action lights the fuse on the bomb that must now explode in the face of Jesus—unless he can diffuse it quickly. The author of this narrative is beginning to set us up for one of the most remarkable events recorded in ancient history—an event stunning in its mercy and remarkable in its wisdom.

Neither Condemning nor Condoning

Jesus begins his response by doing something strange. He writes on the ground (**v 6**), and then does so again in **verse 8**. It is useless to speculate what he wrote for we do not know. We do not need to imagine he actually wrote sentences as such; it could be that he doodled on the ground or drew in the sand. The point seems to be—especially as the action is repeated at another dramatic moment—that Jesus is doing this to heighten the tension. He is increasing the drama. It would be like someone being asked a very difficult question in a seminar, and that person responding by bending over their desk with a pen in hand and starting to scribble somewhat randomly on the piece of paper in front of them, to a growing silence, so that the silence that awaits the response becomes almost painful in its intensity.

And so Jesus delivers his famous line into this highly charged atmosphere: "Let any one of you who is without sin be the first to throw a stone at her" (**v 7**). The response is that they start to drift away (**v 9**), as Jesus averts his gaze by once more continuing to write on the ground (**v 8**). The general point of Jesus' statement may be that no one is without sin and therefore they are unable to judge. It may also be more specific—that they have been guilty of the same crime too, especially when we consider Jesus' teaching in the Sermon on the Mount that adultery is not only physical, but a matter of the eye and of the heart too (Matthew 5:27-28).

Finally Jesus speaks directly to the woman caught in adultery. It is a much-misunderstood dialogue. Jesus asks her where her accusers have all gone, and whether anyone has condemned her (John **8:10**). The woman replies that no one has (**v 11**)—because, in light of Jesus' challenge in **verse 7**, no one can. In fact, there is only one person there who is "without sin"—and he now says to this woman, "Neither do I condemn you."

This has often been misunderstood to mean that Jesus does not take a stand against unrighteousness, whether of a sexual or other kind. But we know that Jesus does. He is against evil, and teaches against it. Perhaps this misinterpretation of this passage is why it was viewed as somewhat dubious by some of the early scribes, and might explain its sketchy manuscript history. But Jesus does not end his conversation with the woman simply by saying that he does not condemn her. He then instructs her, "Go now and leave your life of sin" (**v 11**). In other words, Jesus is drawing a line in the sand (is that what he was doing as he scribbled in the dirt?), and telling the woman that she is to repent and live life differently now. Jesus is doing what he does to all repentant sinners: giving them a chance to start again, calling them to change, with no need for them to be condemned for what is condemnable because of his death for sins on the cross.

> We are not to permit sin to continue, but we are also not to condemn sinners.

I wonder whether in our ministries and churches we manage to keep the same balance as Jesus evidences here. We are not to permit sin to continue ("Go now and leave your life of sin"), but we are also not to condemn sinners ("Neither do I condemn you"). Instead, we are called to provide a culture and a context in which we may all start again. This story, whatever its manuscript origin, is a powerful lesson in the need to do that, even with those most controversial sexual sins. Milne sums it up very helpfully:

> "The sword of judgment is double-edged. In judging others we judge ourselves, and an unwillingness to pronounce judgment on ourselves undercuts our right to pronounce it on others. Put more generally, God's call to all of us, all of the time, is to live

holy, godly lives. Any deviation from that should concern us, as much in ourselves as in others." (*John*, page 125)

The Light of the World

Jesus now, in **verse 12**, utters one of his great statements of identity: "I am the light of the world." He has shone his light upon the darkness of the Pharisees, and lit up the darkness of the woman caught in adultery. Jesus' use of language that reminds us of John's Prologue shows how much John drew upon Jesus' own words in his framing of that Prologue. Jesus himself taught that he was the light of the world. Those who believe in him will never walk in darkness. The theological and practical meanings of this great metaphor are not spelled out in detail, though they certainly include purpose and eternal life within their implications: the release from the darkness of sin and the promise of life forevermore with Jesus as our light. But the metaphor itself has a way of speaking about these profound matters as it reverberates within the souls of those who read about it and hear it spoken.

Not so with the Pharisees. With barely a heartbeat allowed to pass after Jesus says "I am the light of the world," they come up with a caviling complaint based upon a form of religious red tape: "Here you are, appearing as your own witness; your testimony is not valid" (**v 13**). They are presumably referring to Deuteronomy 17:6, where Moses taught that matters of truth needed to be established by two or three witnesses. However, there Moses was talking about someone not being condemned to death without two or three witnesses. It is strange that they would apply this here to Jesus' claim. But perhaps they are now so fixed in a mindset of trying to convict Jesus and send him to death that any text that may relate to that is at the front of their minds. Or perhaps they are thinking of the general principle of needing other witnesses beyond merely one. But what they are not doing is seeing and savoring Jesus:

"It is a most beautiful title of Christ when he is called the light of the world. We are all blind by nature, but a remedy is offered to rescue and free us from darkness and make us partakers of the true light. And this blessing is not offered just to one here or there, for Christ says that he is the light of the whole world."

(John Calvin, *Calvin's New Testament Commentaries,* Vol. 1, page 210)

Jesus makes a great and beautiful statement of positive truth; and they find the text that will have the most negative effect they can think of on Jesus' claims, and which does not even really apply to the situation, but they use that to avoid even considering what he is claiming.

Jesus, though, graciously plays along, and replies according to their objection. What humility it must have taken for the Son of God himself to play these sorts of games with third-rate scholars! In John **8:14-18**, Jesus makes three points in reply to their objection.

First, even if he is witnessing to himself, that does not undermine his witness, because he knows where he came from and where he is going (**v 14**). Here there is a hint of a deep principle of philosophy and **systematic theology**. If God is God, then no other higher authority can be appealed to in order to prove that he is God, for then that other higher authority is really God. This is **circular reasoning**, to be sure, but it is not viciously circular, because Jesus will provide other reasons too; still, it needs to be said. As God incarnate, he does know what he is talking about!

Second, Jesus makes the point that they are thinking wrongly about this because they are still being judgmental (**v 15**). Of course, there is a sense in which Jesus himself is making a discerning judgment about himself, and other people, when he says that he is the "light of the world" (**v 12**). But if and when Jesus judges (**v 16**; see 5:22), his judgment is true because it is the judgment of both himself and the Father (**8:16**).

Third, there is another witness: namely, God the Father. Jesus allows the rule of two witnesses to stand for the sake of argument (**v 17**), and then he offers the other witness—his Father (**v 18**). Once again he is hinting that ultimate truth statements can be based only on the authority of the ultimate Person—that is, on God himself.

The Pharisees completely miss the point of what he is saying, whether willfully or not. "Where is your father?" they ask (**v 19**), expecting some man to appear from the crowd. But Jesus keeps on hammering away at his claims that he is God himself and that his Father is the Father God: "If you knew me, you would know my Father also." The beginnings of a trinitarian approach are being expressed in these few words. To know Jesus is to know the Father God as well, for both are fully God and God is one. With such a bold claim you would expect uproar in response, but because his "hour had not yet come" (that is, the cross, which looms over every part of John's Gospel with increasing clarity now as the story progresses), no one does anything (**v 20**). When Jesus is crucified, it will be his time according to his plan, when his "hour" has come. He will die not according to their agenda, but God's.

Missing the Point

From **verse 21**, Jesus begins to increase the clarity of his "light" to an even more intense level: "I am going away, and you will look for me, and you will die in your sin." You would think that such a statement would cause shock and horror among those who were listening: "you will die in your sin." But instead, once again, they entirely miss his point, wondering whether he is going to commit suicide (**v 22**). At least they are beginning to realize that Jesus is talking about death, but they have no concept of what he means in any profound or significant sense. So Jesus tries again, this time describing the situation with devastating distinctions between their origin in this "world" and his divine origin "not of this world", between their worldliness and his godliness, between their fallenness and his purity. "You are from below; I am from above. You are of this world; I am not of this world. I told you that you would die in your sins; if you do not believe that I am he, you will indeed die in your sins" (**v 23-24**).

Jesus is calling for faith, and they still wonder what on earth he could mean; they seek intellectual clarity and hide in religious debate. "Who are you?" they ask him (**v 25**). This is not completely dim-witted, but by this point it is close to it.

There is a possibility that in what Jesus has said, he is making a startling claim, which further underlines his claim to be "the light of the world." When he tells them that they must believe that "I am he" (**v 28**), he is saying they must believe that "I am," a form of words that would have reminded the attentive listener of Yahweh, the great I AM (as we have seen before, 4:26). That is perhaps why, in reply to their dim-witted question ("Who are you?"), Jesus replies, "Just what I have been telling you from the beginning" (**8:25**). They have heard it over and over again. They do not need it to be repeated; they just need to truly "hear" what has already been told to them.

In **verse 26**, Jesus summarizes his authoritative claim to be able to make ultimate truth statements about himself and others. Rather than being judged by them concerning his identity ("Who are you?" **v 25**), really he has much he could say or judge about who they are (**v 26**). Yet for now, at least, he is not primarily there to judge; he is there, on his Father's authority, to "tell the world" of salvation by faith in him.

They still do not understand (**v 27**). And so Jesus says again, referring to his death, "When you have lifted up the Son of Man [that is Jesus himself], then you will know that I am he" (**v 28**), or "that I AM." This came to pass, as recorded in Acts 2, on the Day of Pentecost, as the seventeenth-century pastor and theologian Matthew Henry pointed out:

> "The guilt of their sin in putting Christ to death would so awaken their consciences that they would be put upon serious enquiries after a Saviour, and then would know that Jesus was he who alone could save them. And so it proved, when, being told that with wicked hands they had crucified and slain the Son of God, they cried out, What shall we do? and were made to know assuredly that this Jesus was Lord and Christ, Acts 2:36."
>
> (*Commentary on the Whole Bible (Matthew to John)*, Vol. 5: commentary on Chapter 8)

Again, Jesus points out that he is not speaking solo. Since the Father and he are one, he speaks as the Father speaks (John **8:28**), and so he has the authority to speak as he does, claiming to be the light of the world, and the I AM of God. The Father is with him. He has not left him (**v 29**). And their relationship is such that the Son always pleases the Father in beautiful communion. Far from being a lone ranger or a radical, difficult prophet who is taking liberties with the Scriptures and with the testimony of God the Father, actually Jesus and God the Father are one. Jesus' bold teaching has an impact. Though some do not understand and do not believe, many do (**v 30**).

Hear Jesus' Words

Perhaps you have been "caught in adultery." Would you hear Jesus' words to "go now and leave your life of sin"? Would you let his light shine on you and walk in that light, in accountability with others, and with a repentant clean conscience, in purity of heart and relationship with Christ?

Perhaps you are listening to all this teaching from Jesus and taking it in thoughtfully. Would you, as you study this Gospel of John—as you hear Jesus saying these things—believe in him?

Perhaps you have friends or colleagues who find it hard to accept that Jesus is God. Would you take fresh courage to speak to them, as well as cultivating great joy in your own faith, from the valid and persuasive way in which Jesus points to the truth of his own claims and the saving power of his person, in this section of John?

Questions for reflection

1. How does Jesus help us to have a high view of sin, and an even higher view of grace? How would this apply, for example, to a member of your church who has committed adultery?

2. How will you look to Jesus as your guiding light today, in a way that you did not, or struggled to, yesterday?

3. How do you need Jesus to tell you today, "Go now and leave your life of sin"?

9. FREE TO SEE THE LIGHT

The question of authority and identity continues to hang over the exchange between Jesus and the Jewish people and leaders that began at the start of chapter 7. That question of who Jesus is still stands as the most important question we could ask ourselves. Our self-identity is only found as we rest in his identity. Our confusions about who we are, why we are here, and what we are meant to do with our lives all increasingly resolve themselves as we see him for who he is, for we are made for him. It's a little like being a hand that is detached from an arm; when the hand "sees" the body for what it really is, and the arm for what it really is, the identity of the detached hand becomes obvious: to be reattached to the arm and become a part of the greater purpose of the body. In somewhat similar fashion, our identity becomes larger (not smaller) when we find ourselves lost in love and wonder and praise for who Jesus is.

Where to Find True Freedom

We have just been told that there were "many" (8:30) who believed in Jesus after the previous conversation—and yet in these same people Jesus now finds that at least some of their faith is less than sincere.

In **8:31**, Jesus begins addressing these people who had expressed some faith in him by instructing them that to be his disciples means not simply making a one-off expression of faith, but "holding" on to this teaching. Jesus does not just ask for commitment; he asks for full-orbed devotion, at the same time as promising those who are truly his disciples that they will "know the truth," and that "the truth will set you free" (**v 32**). What exactly Jesus meant by this has long been debated. Several observations are worth making.

It is clear from Jesus' statement that truth is not merely intel-lectual. To know the truth requires a commitment to the Person of truth: to Jesus himself. This point has been forgotten by much of the Western intellectual establishment at its peril. Intellectual achieve-ment is good and learning is useful; but learning needs, if it is not to be foolish, to be combined with moral commitment to Jesus himself. Mottoes from the old universities recognized this: Yale University's historic motto is *Lux et Veritas*. Truth (*veritas*) requires the light (*lux*) of commitment to Christ.

Further, Jesus is teaching that understanding the truth about him has a practical and personal freeing impact. We should not be those who think that truth is an intellectual game with no implications for real life. Quite the contrary: it is the truth that sets you free. Many people are bound by bonds they do not understand, and the first step to being released is to understand the truth of their situation and the truth of Jesus as the solution. Such truth is not merely indi-vidualistic or self-projected—not merely my truth but *the* truth. Truth is in fact a Person, and a relationship with him is how we come to the truth. And once we trust him, then (at a personal level) the truth sets us free.

What We're Freed From

This sounds like great news—Jesus' listeners, however, are offended (**v 33**). They argue that, as they are Abraham's children, they have never been the slaves of anyone—therefore they do not need to be set free. It would be hard to conceive of any statement more ridiculous. This claim is being made in a country that is under the dominion of Rome, by a people who have only relatively recently returned from captivity in Babylon. They, if anyone, should surely realize that their national descent from Abraham has not kept them from slavery! Since they do not, we can only expect them to be still more offended by Jesus' next statement, as he goes beyond or beneath these political matters to their root cause: sin. "Very truly I tell you, everyone who sins is a slave to sin" (**v 34**).

As ever, Jesus manages to summarize a profound truth in simple terms, in a way that continues to find echoes in the most complex analyses of human personality. Addictive behaviors—the way in which repeated actions create channels in the physiological and biochemical architecture of our minds—are all reflective of this simple statement: that whoever sins is a slave to sin. Habits are not easily broken, and when they are sinful habits, they spiral down into slavery. We may feel we choose to sin but, in fact, that sin is our master.

> We may feel we choose to sin but, in fact, that sin is our master.

But the truth will set us free, and so the truth immediately offers hope. A slave has no "permanent place" in the family, whereas a son does (**v 35**). Jesus is "the Son," and so, if he sets you free, "you will be free indeed" (**v 36**). Jesus is offering freedom from the slavery of sin. What a wonderful prospect of hope it is that he holds before the eyes of those around him! Anticipating their renewed objection, that they are Abraham's children already and not slaves to sin, he reminds them that they are not acting like Abraham's children (**v 37-38**), whereas he is behaving as the Father God has instructed him, and so is showing himself to be the true Son of God.

They fire back with the simple objection: "Abraham is our father" (**v 39**). Jesus makes his point even clearer: Abraham's true children would do what Abraham did (**v 39**). But they are trying to kill him— which is not what Abraham would do (**v 40**), so they are not really Abraham's children. Jesus does not dispute their physical heritage. He is saying that spiritually they are in slavery. They are displaying characteristics of a quite different kind of "father" than Abraham (**v 41**—Jesus picks up on this again in **v 44**).

In response to being told that Jesus' Father is God (**v 38**) and that they are not true children of Abraham (**v 40-41a**), they object that God himself is their Father too (**v 41b**). *Not at all*, says Jesus. If God were their Father, they would love Jesus because he has come from God (**v 42**).

Notice what Jesus is saying: how someone treats him is how they treat God the Father. Because Jesus is God's Son, has been sent by God and represents God, and is God, then to say that we love God but do not love Jesus is actually to say that we do not love God. When someone loves God and they hear about Jesus, they will immediately love Jesus. There is no other possibility since Jesus is the true Son of God. God is not the Father of those who do not love and obey his Son.

Raising the Stakes

But none of this makes any difference to those who by now are growing angry with Jesus; they have a spiritual deafness and so are "unable to hear" what he says (**v 43**). They hear it physically, but they do not really hear it; they do not get it. Jesus now makes his point crystal clear (**v 44**): their father is the devil. What a thing to say! Anyone who thinks that Jesus is always "meek and mild" and never willing to offend anyone should read this passage. Because they are rejecting Jesus—indeed, they are seeking to destroy him and lying about it—the only conclusion must be that really they are following the instructions of the enemy of Jesus and of his Father: that is, of the devil himself. They are opposed to the truth (**v 45**):

> "When we bear in mind the meaning of 'truth' in this Gospel, where the concept finds its embodiment in Jesus himself, it follows that for his disciples to know the truth they must not only hear his words: they must in some sort be united with him who is the truth." (F. F. Bruce, *The Gospel of John,* pages 196-197)

We should note in this context that Jesus believes in a real devil. He is not a medieval caricature with horns and tail; he is real and far more dangerous than that cartoon figure of fun. The devil exists, and there really are people who serve his agenda. Such people need rescuing; they need the gospel. They are to be loved and witnessed to—not ostracized—in the hope they will be saved. But the reality of the spiritual war against Jesus and his word is here made quite clear. Jesus' opponents cannot "prove" him "guilty of sin" (**v 46**), and yet they are trying to kill him. They will not listen to him. Jesus tells them, "The reason you do not hear is that you do not belong to God" (**v 47**):

> "The truth of which Jesus speaks [in John 8] is the revelation which comes from the Father and is passed on in the word of Jesus. To become true disciples of Christ, one must not only believe in his words, one must also continue in his word; his word must find room in one's heart."
>
> (Hamid-Khani, *Revelation and Concealment of Christ,* page 343)

Whose Side is the Devil On?

Having been called out as those who are following the devil, the Jewish people arguing with Jesus now turn the tables on Jesus and say that he is actually the one who is demonic! "Aren't we right in saying that you are a Samaritan and demon-possessed?" (**v 48**). Notice that they combine being a Samaritan with being demon-possessed. Since the Samaritans were considered the enemy within, perhaps Jesus is called demon-possessed because his successful ministry among the Samaritans back in chapter 4 has now been reported back to them. If the Samaritans like Jesus (the argument goes), that just goes to show that he's devilish!

Jesus has tried to show them that their spiritual situation is genuinely serious; to reject the accusation, they resort to name-calling and spiritual mudslinging. It was one of the most common tactics against Jesus. He tried to save prostitutes: he must be immoral. He was a friend of sinners: he must be a sinner. He had a ministry to Samaritans: he must be from the devil's own country.

In **verse 49**, Jesus simply denies that he is demon-possessed. Why is that so clear? Because, he says, "I honor my Father." The one who honors God cannot by definition be demon-possessed, any more than the one who promotes the good of a particular country and honors it and seeks its prosperity can in any credible way be charged with being its enemy. Jesus is clearly on the side of God, and therefore he is not demon-possessed.

They "dishonor" him by calling him by such names, and yet Jesus will still be honored, not because he seeks his own honor, but because God the Father seeks it (**v 50**). How will Jesus still receive honor despite their attacks on him? By the fact that whoever believes in Jesus and obeys his word "will never see death" (**v 51**).

Of all the remarkable statements in this conversation, it is this one that appears to strike the original hearers as most remarkable. Understandably so: imagine if you met someone today who made this claim—that if you obey his word, you will never die.

> Though Jesus' people die, yet they will live forever.

Jesus, of course, does not mean physical death here (all his followers in every generation between his and ours have died). He is saying that though his people die, yet they will live forever (see 11:25-26). "Death" in the Bible is more than—though it includes—the physical cessation of the beating human heart or the decay of our physical matter. "Death" is separation from God eternally. That is why, when Adam and Eve were expelled from the Garden of Eden, they "died" at that moment, though their physical death took place much later (Genesis 3:22-24; 5:5). Similarly, once we have been reconciled to God through obeying Jesus' word, we will never die. Our bodies, unless Jesus returns beforehand, will die and decay—but we will go to be with him forever, and when he returns, our bodies will be renewed and rise again to dwell in the new heaven and the new earth.

Understandably enough, those around Jesus do not grasp all this (John **8:52-53**). That he was saying such outrageous things appears to be sure proof that he is indeed demon-possessed. Remember C.S. Lewis' famous trilemma (see page 101): for a man to say that he is God can only mean one of three things: either he is mad, bad, or he is indeed who he says he is. At least now they are grasping the magnitude of Jesus' claim to be God, though they are coming to the conclusion that he is "bad," and not that he is who he claims to be. So, having noted that even Abraham and all the prophets died, they demand, "Who do you think you are?" (**v 53**).

This is the very question Jesus wants them, and us, to ask and to answer. Who is Jesus? Who is this person who is making these shocking, outrageous, astonishing claims about himself, and about what he will do for those who follow his word? Who do you say that Jesus is?

Jesus sidesteps the question a little. "If I glorify myself, my glory means nothing" (**v 54**). Instead, he is seeking the glory that comes from the "Father," which will be revealed more and more through his ministry, and finally proven at his resurrection from the dead. But, says Jesus, he will not deny the conclusion at which they are driving; if he said he did not know the Father, he would be lying (**v 55**).

What he is trying to find is a way of saying what is true in a manner that will help them to be able to accept it, despite them increasingly showing themselves as his enemies (remember, they started this part of the conversation professing belief, back in **verses 30-31**). So he comes back to what Abraham thought and said. Accepting for a moment their claim that Abraham is their father, he tells them, "Your father Abraham rejoiced at the thought of seeing my day; he saw it and was glad" (**v 56**).

What does Jesus mean by saying that Abraham saw his day and was glad? The answer that appears to hold most warrant is the traditional one: that Abraham "saw the LORD" or the "angel of the LORD"

(Genesis 18:16-33; 22:1-19) and that Jesus is saying that these meetings were pre-incarnate encounters with himself. It is interesting that they are mediatory—that is, about God providing a way out of judgment via sacrifices that rescue both **Lot** and **Isaac**. In that sense, Abraham saw more than perhaps we would have at first realized.

Those standing around in Jesus' day are shocked by his apparent arrogance, if not insanity: "You are not yet fifty years old ... and you have seen Abraham!" (John **8:57**). Surely Jesus is showing himself as crazy or malevolent, and certainly not as God, by these kinds of claims. Yet Jesus goes to his great final statement, and one of the most famous utterances of his divinity: "Very truly I tell you ... before Abraham was born, I am!" (**v 58**). The resonance of the "I am" statements throughout this chapter now come to a resounding conclusion. Jesus is claiming to be the I AM, Yahweh, God, the eternal one. In case any think that Jesus did not quite imply all of this, and that we might be reading too much into the text, we need only note the response of his first hearers: "They picked up stones to stone him" (**v 59**). They knew that Jesus was saying he was God.

Bow Before Him

Recognizing Jesus as God changes our lives—as long as it is not merely an intellectual recognition, but rather a personal acceptance of, and a relationship with, the truth that sets us free. In other words, to be set free we need to recognize that truth as *the* truth, and bow before Jesus, not as merely another moral teacher but as the great I AM: as God. Would you spend a moment bowing before Jesus as God? Would you spend a moment asking yourself whether your life is being lived for Jesus, or whether your life is being lived for yourself? Are you functionally acting as if there is a more important truth than this person, and a way to be set free other than this one? It is only when we trust in Christ as the Truth more and more each day that we are set free.

Questions for reflection

1. How have you experienced the reality that knowing Jesus and obeying his teaching is what delivers true freedom?

2. If it is "the truth" that sets us free, what implications does this have for the relativistic mindset of Western society, where everyone's truth is thought to be equally valid?

3. In what ways do people today seek to escape the binary choice that Jesus leaves us with, between acknowledging him as the eternal God or concluding that he is a charlatan?

PART TWO

Sometimes the most apparently "enlightened" people are less insight-ful than those who have been less well educated or instructed. There's none so foolish as an educated fool, as the saying goes. While learning can give genuine light, it does not necessarily allow us to be wise, or spiritually insightful, or give what we often call "common sense." What does it take to really "see" the meaning of life, and "perceive" the best way to live life? Our story in this part is all about sight and blindness.

A Blind Man Meets the Light

There is a blind man, and Jesus is passing by (**9:1**). Notice how Jesus "saw" him. Is there here a suggestion that Jesus did not merely see him out of the corner of his eye, but observed him—had compassion upon him as he contemplated him?

The disciples ask, "Rabbi, who sinned, this man or his parents, that he was born blind?" (**v 2**). They are assuming that all personal suf-fering is a direct result of personal sin. Evidently, they are not too familiar with the story of **Job** in the Old Testament, or they would not be making the same mistake that **Job's "comforters"** did (Job 16:2). While it is certainly true that all suffering is a result of the fall, and so a consequence of sin in general, it is not true that therefore there is a direct line between an individual's personal, moral failure and an individual's personal suffering.

This truth is implied in Jesus' answer, for this man's blindness exists so that the works of God might be displayed in him (John **9:3**). What higher calling could there be? It would have shocked those listening as much as it perhaps shocks us to think that God's saving power might be displayed in a suffering person, rather than a successful person. F.F. Bruce underlines just what kind of glory will be revealed in what is about to happen to this man:

"The healing of the blind man is presented as a **parable** of spiritual illumination. Thanks to the coming of the true light of the

world, many who were formerly in darkness have been enlightened; this is not only the effect but the purpose of his coming."

(*The Gospel of John*, page 220)

Jesus then defines what he means by "works," emphasizing that it is
his saving mission and purpose, given to him by the Father (**v 4**). The
point is that this man's life has been specifically designed, suffering
and all, and this encounter with Jesus specifically arranged. It is not
haphazard in the slightest, but intended to reveal the purpose of Jesus' mission to the world. When he says, "Night is coming, when no
one can work," Jesus is pointing us to an eternal perspective: there
is a mission which we can accomplish now which in glory we cannot:
namely, evangelism leading to eye-opening salvation. This is the one
thing that we can do now that we cannot do in the new heaven and
new earth—the "work" of witnessing to Christ as the "light of the
world" (8:12), so that people might be saved. The statement functions as a clarion call for disciples to focus upon the core task of evangelism before "night" comes—the night of judgment and separation
from God for those who do not believe in Jesus.

This is why, at the end of **9:5**, Jesus once again says, "I am the
light of the world." This context makes clear the primary focus of that
statement. The story of the blind man being healed will illustrate who
"sees" that Jesus is the light and who does not "see." Jesus has come
that those who are blind may see (and to make clear who truly are
"blind" even though they think they can "see").

Perfect Vision, but Total Blindness

Now we come, in **verse 6**, to a strange moment when Jesus appears
to give what some have thought are pseudo-medical instructions,
when surely, as the Son of God, he need only say, "See!" for the man
to be able to see. Jesus does elsewhere heal in such a dramatic way
(Mark 5:30; Luke 7:9-10), but not here. Instead he makes mud with
saliva, puts it on the man's eyes, and tells him to wash in the Pool of
Siloam (John **9:7**). Unlike the case of the deaf-mute (Mark 7:33), we

cannot say that this was because otherwise he would not have known what Jesus was about to do. The man here in John 9 could not see but he could hear, and so he could receive instructions.

John tells us that this word "Siloam" means "Sent" (John **9:7**). Why the added detail? Perhaps because we are meant to see Jesus' message through "sending" this man to the pool and healing him as a missional "sending" message to those around.

What about the mud and saliva (**v 6**)? This could be Jesus' way of confirming what he has already told them: namely, that this man's congenital blindness was not because he or his parents had done something morally wrong. On this understanding, Jesus is showing that in fact this is a medical matter (as we would put it), even though he is going to employ a supernatural solution. Saliva at the time was believed to hold basic healing properties (as indeed it is still today, as mothers the world over will testify). Jesus makes a very basic pharmaceutical paste, not because he wants the man to think that Jesus is a medical doctor or that the man is receiving a medical solution to his condition (the man very clearly understands he has been miraculously healed, as the story will show), but because Jesus wants the man, his parents, and Jesus' own disciples, as well as us today, to realize that the man's blindness was not his own moral fault. Rather, it was designed for this purpose: to reveal Jesus as the Light of the world. Jesus does not have the man confess his sins. He makes it clear this is a purely physical healing.

Next we enter into the part of the story—and there are several of these—that has real comedy value. Passages like this in Scripture reveal the all-too-frequently funny side of our own spiritual shortsightedness. In **verse 8**, we see the neighbors asking around about what has happened, wanting to know whether this fully-seeing man, who looks remarkably like a blind man they know, can actually be the same person. The only possible solution to their conundrum (after all, how can God heal those born blind?!) is that it is a case of mistaken identity. But they disagree among themselves. Then in comes the previously blind man, who actually says, "I am the man" (**v 9**). Can you see the humor in how he has to keep on saying that he is the same person who once was blind? He has to insist.

Of course, they want to know how he is now able to see (**v 10**). He tells them it was Jesus, and explains the procedure (**v 11**). Then they want to know where Jesus is (**v 12**). But now he doesn't know where Jesus is—he can't see him, even though he can now see. It's like a Monty Python sketch: "The *Blind* Parrot," perhaps.

In the way of the religiously blind the world over, the people's first response when they realize they have a genuine miracle on their hands is to take it to the authorities to have it assessed (**v 13**). There is nothing wrong in the authoritative assessment, in and of itself, but the real problem they have is exposed by John in **verse 14**, when he tells his readers that this happened on the Sabbath. A dramatic work of God on the Sabbath—we'll have to put a stop to that!

So in **verse 15** the assessment process begins with the Pharisees asking how the man is now able to see. You get the feeling straightaway that they want to discover a problem. They are looking for difficulties, not rejoicing in healing. And perhaps we would respond in the same way today…

> The Pharisees fail to see anything but their own assumptions.

The man recounts, again, his story. Despite all the carefully enacted approach to this healing that Jesus has performed, the one detail that the Pharisees grasp is that this took place on the Sabbath (**v 16**). God's people were not meant to work on the Sabbath—and surely this was some kind of work. In their eyes, Jesus' shockingly slipshod approach to the Sabbath is deeply offensive. But Jesus is showing that the whole point of the Sabbath is to set people from slavery, and so the healing is part of the point of Sabbath ministry—if only they could or would see it.

Some of the Pharisees immediately fail to see anything but their own assumptions: Jesus certainly cannot be "from God," yet, "How can a sinner perform such signs?" (**v 16**). Their assembly is divided, and so—in an astonishing admission of weakness—they ask the previously blind man his own opinion (**v 17**).

The man replies that Jesus is a prophet. No answer is given to this obvious, if incomplete, conclusion at this point. But plainly, the Pharisees do not like the logic which the man's conclusion represents. They look for another way out: perhaps it is a case of mistaken identity after all! So they send for his parents (**v 18**), and ask them whether he is actually their son (**v 19**)—and, if he is, how on earth it is that he is now able to see. His parents confirm that, yes, this is their boy (**v 20**), but (reasonably enough) they say they don't know how he came to see, and that really the Pharisees should ask him as he is old enough to answer (**v 21**). John explains that this was not simple reasoning but an attempt to pass the buck, because his parents knew that if they looked to be siding with Jesus or affirming him as the Christ or Messiah, they were risking expulsion from the synagogue (**v 22-23**).

So, again, the Pharisees summon the man (the blind parrot sketch continues) and ask him again about the whole matter (**v 24**). Now, however, the stakes are raised. The Pharisees' council is getting fed up, and they want to hear the answer that they want to hear, and so they say, "Give glory to God"—a way of saying, *As you swear by Almighty God, tell us the truth*. In effect, they wheel out the biggest, blackest, oldest Bible they can find, make him put his hand on it, and compel him to promise to "tell the truth, the whole truth, and nothing but the truth, so help me God." This puts the formerly blind man in a very difficult position when the question comes—because the question is not really a question: "We know this man is a sinner" (**v 24**). Here is the definition of a leading question (or, to be precise, a leading non-question): *Okay, tell us the truth, so help you God—and by the way, this is the answer we expect you to give, the only "truth" we want you to tell us.* Who is really "blind" and who is really a "sinner" is becoming more and more apparent as the story progresses.

In words made world-famous by the eighteenth-century slave-trader who became a pastor and hymn-writer, John Newton, the man, determined not to get caught in that trap, says that he knows only one thing: "I was blind but now I see" (**v 25**).

Amazing grace, how sweet the sound,
That saved a wretch like me,
I once was lost but now am found,
Was blind but now I see.

Who could argue with that? And because they cannot, the Pharisees now resort to the time-honored tactics of the bully caught in a logical trap: they start to insult him instead of arguing with him (**v 28**). In the midst of their abuse, the issue that sticks in their throats is revealed again: they know where Moses came from, but not where Jesus came from (**v 29**). Behind this lies the fact that it is not Jesus' geographical origin that preoccupies them, but the source of his authority—whether he is from God or from the devil. The once-blind man will have none of it though (**v 30**); he tells them that their inability to decide whether Jesus is from God or not is ridiculous, given what Jesus has done.

The Right Response

This Jesus now appears again on the scene, having sought and found the man who had been born blind because Jesus has heard that he has been expelled from the synagogue (**v 34-35**). As a pariah now, alone and friendless in a highly religious society, the man is deeply vulnerable. Jesus does not leave him in that state. But instead of merely comforting him, he immediately asks him a question: "Do you believe in the Son of Man?" (**v 35**). The man's answer is fascinating (**v 36**). Given who Jesus is and what Jesus has done for him, he is now willing to believe what Jesus tells him. How different than the Pharisees! "Who is he, sir? ... Tell me so that I may believe in him." And then Jesus tells him that this Son of Man is himself (**v 37**). The man throws himself on his face and worships Jesus (**v 38**). Here, at last, after all the deliberate refusal to listen to truth or respond to evidence, is the right response to Jesus.

Now comes one of Jesus' great purpose statements. **Verse 39** shows that the image of Jesus as everyone's friend has always been wrong. We need to get on Jesus' side, rather than assume that Jesus will support whatever it is we want to do. As the great US President Abraham Lincoln once replied during the American Civil War, when told by someone that God was on their side: "Sir, my concern is not whether God is on our side; my greatest concern is to be on God's side, for God is always right." Jesus' purpose is saving ("the blind will see"); but because some will refuse Jesus, his purpose is also judgment (those who see—or, rather, think that they see but really do not—will become blind). Leon Morris sums it up well:

> The image of Jesus as everyone's friend has always been wrong.

"John evidently wants us to see that the activity of Jesus as the Light of the world inevitably results in judgment on those whose natural habitat is darkness."

(*The Gospel According to John*, page 429)

The Pharisees seem to realize that this general statement could apply to them (**v 40**)—if the hat fits, wear it! So now Jesus finally reveals the point of this whole discussion: they are the blind ones. Physical blindness, like this man had suffered, is not a sign that someone is guilty of sin, (**v 41**). But because they claim that they can see (their shocked tone at any suggestion that they might be blind makes it clear that they think they can see), it proves that actually they are blind, spiritually speaking—and that makes them guilty. Their religious arrogance has blinded them to any possibility of seeing their own sin, and therefore to seeing their need of Jesus.

Religious Pride and Spiritual Blindness

It is humbling to read in this story how, once again, it is the religiously well-informed who fail to be transformed by "seeing" a miracle done by Jesus himself. How do we guard ourselves against the spiritual pride that can "blind" us to truly seeing and experiencing God? Sometimes it is easier to spot the symptoms of pride than cure the disease. The great eighteenth-century American preacher Jonathan Edwards put it like this:

> "One under the influence of spiritual pride is more apt to instruct others, than to inquire for himself, and naturally puts on the airs of a master. Whereas one that is full of pure humility, naturally has on the air of a disciple."
>
> (*Thoughts on the New England Revival,* Vol. I, page 402)

Notice how the religious leaders here refuse to be instructed. But the most important component of a faithful (and humble) Bible teacher, as well as a student, is the willingness—in fact the desire, the longing—to learn.

It would be easy to say that the real cure for spiritual pride is a good long look in the mirror; except for the truth that, according to James, it is easy to look in the mirror of God's word and ignore what we see there (James 1:23). This is what we see in John 9: the Pharisees look directly at Jesus, hear him personally, and yet still remain blind to who he really is; they still walk away no wiser and more guilty (John **9:41**).

What does it take for us to be healed of our blindness? That is revealed by the experience of another supremely and zealously proud Pharisee. Saul of Tarsus also persecuted Jesus, through persecuting his disciples. But by God's grace, his religious pride was broken by an encounter with Jesus (Acts 9:3-9). There, he finally saw the truth, even as he became physically blind and then physically restored. Having been humbled, he responded to God's call to a life of servitude and suffering, and through such a life God gradually worked out of him the remaining elements of pride, until he had run the race and fought the good fight (2 Timothy 4:7). We, then, whoever we are and however zealous or intellectually sharp we may be, need to defeat our religious pride; or rather, to have it defeated for us, in us. And we win that victory and experience that defeat if and as we have a personal encounter with Christ, recognizing him, allowing him to show us where we are mistaken, and experiencing with him an ongoing life of joyful, and costly, discipleship.

Questions for reflection

1. If the Pharisees teach us anything, it is that religious pride is a great and real danger. How can we guard ourselves against it?

2. What does this section tell us to expect as those who have seen Jesus for who he is and therefore follow him as Lord?

3. How does Jesus' treatment of the ex-blind man, and his confrontation with the religious bullies, reveal Jesus' character? How will you worship him for who he is right now?

10. THE GREATEST SHEPHERD

We come now to one of the most familiar scenes, and analogies, in the Bible: Jesus as the good shepherd. Those who grew up in church, or are familiar with traditional church language, or have heard a sermon or two, are likely as not to have become acquainted with the metaphor that Jesus uses throughout this famous passage. It is certainly a beautiful picture; a shepherd looking after sheep is a romanticized scene in many cultures and societies. However, though it is indeed a beautiful scene, it is also a costly role.

In fact, that issue of cost, in particular of sacrifice, is right at the heart of what Jesus is saying. The good shepherd is one who lays down his life for the sheep (**10:11, 15, 17-18**). That distinctive attribute is the key to us understanding the meaning of the passage, rather than its pastoral sweetness merely resonating with us. Later on (21:15-17), we will see the risen Jesus telling Peter to shepherd Jesus' own sheep—and the key distinctive for Peter, as a true undershepherd, will also be self-sacrifice. If you are called to "shepherd" God's people in one way or another, then you are called to lay down your life for the sheep—not necessarily making the ultimate sacrifice that Jesus did, but still really and actually and daily giving up what is easiest for you. If you are being shepherded by a faithful pastor, then respect and honor such, who give their lives to serve you.

As well as the constant reference to the cross, the other critical feature that distinguishes the true shepherd is the character of a shepherd himself. In the Bible, before Jesus the single most famous shepherd was King David. "Shepherd" does not merely mean a hard-working farmhand or cowboy type; it means royalty. Speaking of the shepherd, Jesus is saying that he is the King, but a sacrificial Shepherd-King—the good shepherd, who lays down his life for the sheep.

Here is Your Shepherd

So let's delve into the sometimes confusing, but always compelling, story of the shepherd and the sheep. And what a shepherd! As Gregory of Nazianzus put it:

"He is the Way, because he leads us through himself. He is the Door who lets us in, the Shepherd who makes us dwell in green pastures, bringing us up by waters of rest and leading us there. He protects us from wild beasts, converts the erring, brings back what was lost and binds up what was broken."

(*Ancient Christian Commentary on Scripture*, *New Testament IV,* page 344)

The metaphors of this Gospel collide and combine to present Jesus in his beauty and glory, as another ancient commentator, Clement of Alexandria, gloriously lays out:

"In our sickness we need a Savior, in our wanderings a guide, in our blindness someone to show us the light, in our thirst the fountain of living water that quenches forever the thirst of those who drink from it. We dead people need life, we sheep need a shepherd, we children need a teacher, the whole world needs Jesus!"

(*Ancient Christian Commentary on Scripture*, *New Testament IV*, page 340)

In **10:1** we begin to see some of the difficulties with this text as we are introduced to the one who "climbs in by some other way." All sorts of possibilities could be and have been suggested, and it is probably stretching credibility too far to suggest that the one who "climbs in by some other way" has to be only one of these. Instead, part of Jesus' picture of what is taking place is probably this: shepherds of their own sheep don't need to climb a wall, any more than the owner of a house needs to climb up the drainpipe to enter. An intruder, thief, or robber tries to break into the house, or, in this case, into the pen where the sheep are kept.

It is, though, crucial to remember the context. Remember, the man born blind has just been thrown out of the synagogue (9:34). So here, Jesus is saying that actually the Pharisees are really not the rightful shepherds. They are wrongly trying to take over the sheep, and by behaving in such a way toward this ex-blind man they are revealing their true nature as thieves and not shepherds. Jesus, on the other hand, is the genuine shepherd of the sheep (**10:2**). What will distinguish the shepherd from a thief will come later (**v 10-11**).

"The gatekeeper" in **verse 3** may have a more specific reference. It is tempting to wonder (though it certainly cannot be proved) whether the "gatekeeper" is actually referring to the man born blind. He now sees Jesus for who he is, so he could be the one who watches for him, and witnesses about him. Or it could be John the Baptist; or the Holy Spirit, opening the door of people's hearts to the ministry of Christ; or it could be that this "gatekeeper" is merely part of the "coloring in" of the illustration, which Jesus is using to make the metaphor more vivid and lifelike. Regardless, the gatekeeper is one who recognizes the true shepherd.

Now, we move on to clearer imagery in this familiar passage (**v 3-4**). The shepherd is distinguished by being the one whose voice the sheep hear and follow, whereas a stranger's voice they will not follow (**v 5**). The way shepherding was (and is still) done in the Middle East was different from the techniques of Britain or Australia. In Britain, sheep are shepherded by means of a sheep dog running behind them and pushing them forward; not so in Jesus' day. The story is told of a tour of Israel, where it had been explained that shepherds there went ahead of the sheep and called to them and they followed. The tour bus went past a person, instead, driving the sheep from behind. One of the tourists pointed this out to the guide, at which point the bus was stopped and the guide hurried off to find out what was going on. A few moments later he reappeared on the tour bus and announced, "He's not the shepherd; he's the butcher." Jesus is the shepherd, not the butcher—he calls his sheep, and they follow. As Carson puts it:

"Unlike Western shepherds who drive the sheep, often using a sheep dog, the shepherds of the Near East, both now and in Jesus' day, lead their flock, their voice calling them on. That such a shepherd goes ahead of his sheep and draws them constitutes an admirable picture of the master/disciple relationship. The sheep follow simply because they know his voice; by the same token, they will run from anyone else because they do not recognize a stranger's voice… Christ's elect sheep inevitably follow him." (John, page 383)

So we need to ask: how do we who follow Jesus today "hear his voice"? The safest possible answer is: through the voice of the Scriptures. Because all Scripture is God-breathed (2 Timothy 3:16), and because Jesus is God, all Scripture is Jesus speaking to us. Certainly, when we come across his specific words spoken while he was physically in Israel, we find a special resonance and meaning in such words (1 Corinthians 7:10, the Lord's own word), but that in no way suggests that the rest of Scripture is not also God's own word (1 Corinthians 7:12) and equally authoritative; in that sense it is just as much Jesus' voice. So the sheep of Jesus will be marked by a characteristic desire to read the Bible, hear the Bible taught, and understand the Bible; not because they are literary eggheads, but because they want to hear the voice of the good shepherd.

> The sheep of Jesus will be marked by a desire to read the Bible, because they want to hear their shepherd's voice.

That said, the Bible itself is also very clear that God speaks in other ways. "The heavens declare the glory of God" (Psalm 19:1), though such "natural revelation" is also clearly limited to revealing his "eternal power" and "divine nature" (not saving revelation): "God's invisible qualities—his eternal power and divine nature—have been clearly seen, being understood from what has been made" (Romans 1:20). There is also a witness of conscience, muddied and buried by the woeful effects of the fall, and further blunted by our own personal depravity; but nonetheless conscience can still cut, and—under the tutelage of the Spirit—softens us to hear from God through his word: "The requirements of the law are written on their hearts, their consciences also bearing witness, and their thoughts sometimes accusing them and at other times even defending them" (Romans 2:15).

So God speaks to us in creation (merely revealing God's nature, not "how to be saved"); in conscience (distorted by the impact of the fall); and then, supremely, in Christ—ultimately and fully, as spoken and heard through the Scriptures. The role of the Spirit in this regard of "hearing the voice of the shepherd" is controversial in **evangelical** circles—those who take a **Pentecostal/charismatic** view differ from those who do not—but all acknowledge that in one way or another the Spirit empowers, convicts, convinces, softens, awakens, counsels, encourages, illumines and points to Jesus (as Jesus himself will teach; see comments on John 14 – 16 in the second volume).

Extravagantly, Expansively Full

The "problem" with this pastoral image is that those listening to Jesus paint the picture with his words do not understand what he is saying (**10:6**)! So Jesus carries on to explain and expand. Now he switches metaphors in a way that would probably frustrate early-education teachers the world over: Jesus is not only the shepherd; he is also "the gate" (**v 7**)! Calvin summed it up helpfully:

> "Christ likens the church to a sheepfold in which God assembles his people, and compares himself to the door, since he is the only entrance into the church."
>
> (*Calvin's New Testament Commentaries,* Vol. 1, page 259)

Those who "have come before"—all the false messiahs and prophets that plagued Israel—did not succeed in leading God's sheep astray (v 8), for only Jesus is the "door", the "gate" (v 9). To enter through him—to believe in him—is the way to be saved; and to carry on in a healthy and growing relationship with God, you "come in and go out" through Jesus and "find pasture." You never move beyond Jesus, or grow out of Jesus, but he gets bigger and more impressive (from your perspective). As the trials you face become more challenging, so your view of him grows by comparison and you go in and out through him, constantly feeding on his word and growing in your faith in him.

The point all this is leading to is this: "The thief comes only to steal and kill and destroy; I have come that they may have life, and have it to the full" (v 10). This text, much beloved of poster-makers for Christian subculture, is undeservedly trivialized, and is truly profound. Jesus' goal for his followers—those who enter through him, "the gate"—is that they would have life, but not just to "be alive" forever in some extended existence of the mediocre or moderately fulfilling. No, he has come to give us life "to the full" or "abundantly" (ESV). The word for "abundantly" has almost the sense of "excessively." It is as if Jesus is saying that the lives of his sheep will not just be middling; they will be extravagantly, expensively, expansively full. Jesus does not promise us that our lives now will be pain-free. No one who follows this good shepherd who gives up his life for the sheep can expect an easy life. But everyone who does follow him is promised a full life. Better to live fully, even at great cost, than never truly to live at all.

The Shepherd v the Wolves

Jesus then returns to his metaphor of himself as the "good shepherd." Now he is starting to make clear what establishes him as this good shepherd. It is that he "lays down his life for the sheep" (v 11), lays down his life for the sheep (v 15), lays down his life for the sheep (v 17), and lays down his life for the sheep (v 18). Any who try to construct a Christian **pastoral ministry** without emphasizing the substitutionary death of Jesus Christ have reckoned without a full understanding of John 10. Jesus' death is "for" the sheep; that is, it is "on account of" or "in place of" or "instead of" or "as a substitute for" the sheep. But we do not need to consult our Greek lexicons to establish this meaning. The point here is that the good shepherd puts his body on the line to protect the sheep from the wolf. He is willing to risk his life, and (as John will later show us) actually does sacrifice his life, to save his sheep. The Lord came as Shepherd-King, not military Emperor:

> "The freedom Jesus wins for his people will be achieved not by sword and shield, but by a cross." (D.A. Carson, *John*, page 385)

The good shepherd knows his own and his own know him—there is an intimacy of relationship and a connection that is the prized gift of grace received by every true follower of Jesus, the good shepherd (**v 14**).

Who is this wolf (**v 12**)? At one level, the wolf is anyone or anything who is trying to kill the sheep. You define wolves not by how big their teeth are (this is not Little Red Riding Hood), but by what they use their teeth for. A wolf, by definition, tries to devour the sheep. But in this immediate context, Jesus probably has specific people in mind too. At this point in the narrative, if anyone is a wolf, it is the Pharisees. Shocking, isn't it? The religious leaders are not praying for their people; they are preying on them. They are not dying on behalf of their people; their people are dying because of them. Be warned, all religious leaders: be dying for your people, or you will be killing them. Sheep are troublesome enough animals, and you will probably have to do one or the other before too long (or get out of the ministry altogether when faced with the choice, like the "hired hand," **v 12-13**).

The "other sheep" from outside "this sheepfold" (**v 16**) is traditionally thought to mean the Gentiles; Jesus desired that all nations would become one as part of his flock. Many have criticized this interpretation as reading into John from later church history. However, we should remember that Jesus has already set an example for what he means by his ministry to the Samaritans in John 4. It is true that in John's Gospel "the world" (1:9-10) does imply "the world in rebellion" and not simply "the whole globe"; but it is also this world that God loves (3:16), and so Jesus' mission is to the whole of rebellious humanity. Here, as in John 4, we see confirmation that the all-nations trajectory of Acts and onwards through the centuries is coherent with Jesus' original intention and mission.

10:17-18 is tricky, and worthy of extended reflection. On the one hand, the Father particularly loves the Son because the Son is going to lay down his life for the sheep. This suggests, at the least, a submission of the Son to the Father. On the other hand, Jesus lays down his life on his own authority and by his own intention (**v 18**). Yet again (if there were a third hand, it would be introduced here), this charge or "command" was received from the Father, which again suggests submission. So God the Father and God the Son have a relationship that may not be quickly quantified and is beyond the reach of mathematics or simplistic logic. We are talking about God, not algebra, and while the Son does submit to the Father's will, the Son also acts on his own initiative since he is fully God too. There is one God (we are here reminded) in two Persons (that's what is being taught here—of course, the Spirit is also one of the Persons of the Trinity, but that is not in view here). They have equal autonomy but distinct roles, and there is a voluntary submission on the part of the Son to the Father.

It is not surprising that the Jews are thrown into a fit of division about this teaching (**v 19**): some think Jesus is mad; others ask (again) how a mad or demon-possessed person can open the eyes of the blind (**v 20-21**; compare 9:16b).

You are a Sheep, You Have a Shepherd

These verses have helped so many people over the years that we do well to pay them due attention. Mark out some space, and take some time, to let the profound truth of Jesus as your good shepherd sink into your heart. It calls you to dependence on Jesus, to listening to his voice, and to following him. It speaks to your need: you are a sheep (a silly, aimless, directionless, wandering sheep). Even the best of us is still a mere sheep. But such humbling realization, which none of us in our honest moments are very far from, is met with a gracious vision of Jesus as this good shepherd, who lays down his life for the sheep.

All shepherds—all under-shepherds/pastors, and all those who shepherd a family—take on this mantle to lay down our lives for the sheep too. That is a hard calling, and it is only made possible by this greater realization that we too are sheep, and we too have a good shepherd to follow; and all (sheep and under-shepherds) who trust in him find him faithful, true, protecting, saving, and suffering for our sake.

Questions for reflection

1. How does seeing Jesus as your good shepherd comfort you, and call you to keep going in your faith, today?

2. How does thinking about shepherding in a Middle-Eastern context help us fully appreciate what Jesus means when he says he is the good shepherd?

3. Are you called to shepherd others? If you are, how does Jesus' shepherding shape your own?

PART TWO

Missing the Wood For The Festive Trees

It is easy to miss the wood for the trees. That is what happens as the "Festival of Dedication" (**10:22**) begins in Jerusalem.

Jesus, we are told, was walking through "Solomon's Colonnade" (**v 23**)—a large covered porch traditionally thought to have stood since the time of Solomon—probably because "it was winter" and this was a shelter against the wind and the cold. "The Festival of Dedication," now commonly known as "Hanukkah," celebrated the rescue of the Jews under the Maccabees and the rededication of the Jerusalem Temple in 165BC. There, walking in the courts, sometime in midwinter, is the one to whom, above all, we and everything in this world should be dedicated, at a time of "dedication." So the question we need to ask is: who will commit themselves to him? As the lights of Hanukkah were playing and the wind howled in winter, the Jewish leaders "gathered around him" (**v 24**). They were reaching decision point: would they or would they not follow Jesus?

It is easy during our own great religious festivals to miss the point that is intended to be celebrated. Perhaps we are busy making arrangements, or organizing the worship experience for others, and too busy to give conscious attention to the one whom we are leading others to worship. Perhaps we are so concerned with what we have to teach—the sermon, or the Bible study, or the Sunday-school class—that we give little time to thinking about what it is that we have to learn. Involvement in religious ceremonies or festivals, however impressive or large or significant the event may be in itself, is not the same as actual engagement with God personally. Mere familiarity, even great awareness, of God is not the same as knowing God. The road to hell is not only paved with the bald heads of friars, as Martin Luther suggested in his commentary on Galatians 2:18—it is also paved with those who have taken on superficial membership of religious institutions, however doctrinally sound the religious institutions themselves may or may not be.

Evidently, the leaders understand that Jesus' very presence in the temple at this festival is posing a question to them, for they turn the question back to him (John **10:24**). The reason they have not made up their minds, they are suggesting, is because Jesus has not been clear enough about his identity. "How long will you keep us in suspense? If you are the Messiah, tell us plainly." *Come on, Jesus! Put us out of our misery—if you are who you say you are, then make it clear.* But the very fact they know who Jesus is claiming to be (the Messiah) exposes as specious their objection that he is not making it clear that he claims to be the Messiah. Of course Jesus has made it clear; that is why they know what he is claiming, and that is also why they are opposing him. Perhaps they were hoping for further evidence of his "blasphemy," so that they might be able to spring a trap and arrest him.

If Jesus was treated like this, we should not be surprised if we are too. A servant is not above his master, and if the Lord of all glory had to deal with knuckleheads deliberately misinter-preting his words, his motives, and his actions, for their own self-serving agenda, we can be sure that we who follow Jesus will face the same sort of knuckleheads ourselves. Martyn Lloyd-Jones would remark on occasion that the greatest opposition that Christians

> The greatest opposition Christians face is not from non-Christians but from fake Christians.

down through the years have faced is not from non-Christians but from fake Christians. So true: any cursory knowledge of the **Reformation**, the **Puritans**, the **Evangelical Awakening**, and twentieth-century Christianity will show that we are more likely to be attacked by the religious than the non-religious. That is not to say that those who are non-religious will not also attack us—especially when they are "religiously non-religious"—zealots with an agenda for their own self-righteousness or self-autonomy, even if their cause is not religiously expressed. Since a servant is not above his master, we are not to be surprised when proclamation of the gospel is confronted by people who claim that our words and actions are **nefarious** and foolish. Such it was with Christ; so it will be with us.

Given that, we need to learn from how Jesus handles opposition. In this instance (though by no means always), Jesus is direct. "I did tell you, but you do not believe" (**v 25**). Jesus' "works" (in John, "works" means his miracles or signs), most recently the miracle of the healing of the man born blind, also tell them who he is. Yet they do not believe. Why not? Jesus' answer is simple: "You are not my sheep" (**v 26**). As the theologian C.K. Barrett puts it:

"The fourth Gospel expresses the conviction that however clearly Jesus may state the truth, those who are not 'his sheep' will not hear his voice." (*Essays on John*, page 107)

The refusal to believe is because these people do not really belong to God. Those who are truly God's people would gather around the Messiah and follow him: "My sheep listen to my voice; I know them, and they follow me" (**v 27**). We are back to Jesus' earlier teaching about the sheep and the shepherd.

Then come two great principles and calming promises. First, "I give them eternal life, and they shall never perish; no one will snatch them out of my hand" (**v 28**). This is a verse to memorize, inscribe on our walls, and drill into our minds. Eternal life is a gift. It is genuinely eternal ("they shall never perish") and it is unchangeable ("no one will snatch them out of my hand"). Waves of relief roll over the disciples of Jesus: they are saved, and they are safe, forever. The nineteenth-century Bishop of Liverpool J.C. Ryle described the encouragement this brings:

"Christ declares that his people 'will never perish'. Weak as they are they will all be saved. Not one of them shall be lost and cast away: not one of them shall miss heaven. If they err, they shall be brought back; if they fall, they shall be raised. The enemies of their soul may be strong and mighty, but their Savior is mightier; and none shall pluck them out of their Savior's hand."

(*Expository Thoughts on the Gospel of John*, page 93)

How many times have we needed the calming, securing, establishing conviction and certainty that come from this promise of our Master: "No one will snatch them out of my hand"? Put in place of that "one" any or all of the "somethings" that seem to you to threaten to snatch you from his hand and out of the realm of his blessing. Money? Money, or the lack of it in poverty, cannot snatch you out of his hand. Sickness? Disease cannot snatch you out of his hand. Rejection? Those we once trusted cruelly rejecting us or betraying us cannot snatch us out of his hand. No trauma, no tragedy, no mountain, no valley can snatch us out of his hand. Rail and shout as the devil may, we are safe in his tender grasp. Christian, believe it.

Unsnatchable

Now comes an explanation. How is this possible? Because "my Father, who has given them to me, is greater than all; no one can snatch them out of my Father's hand" (**v 29**). So, because the Father has given Jesus his sheep, no one can take them away, since the Father is the Father God and he is "greater than all."

Immediately, given the resonance and repetition of "no one will snatch them out of my hand" followed by "no one can snatch them out of my Father's hand," there is an association of identity and an equality of power and person. Here, Jesus makes this implication (frequently present in the Gospels in what Jesus says and does) quite explicit: "I and the Father are one" (**v 30**).

There is no way to explain away or scale down that claim. The Jews get that. "Again his Jewish opponents picked up stones to stone him" (**v 31**). They must have been tired of scouring around for suitably sized stones only for Jesus' quick reply to stop them in their tracks (**v 32**): "I have shown you many good works from the Father. For which of these do you stone me?" *What is the charge and basis for this act of execution?* he asks. *Are you killing me because I healed someone?* The Jewish leaders reply that it is not for his works or miracles, but because of what he is claiming: it is "blasphemy, because you, a mere man, claim to be God" (**v 33**).

At this point it is worth stopping and realizing what a theological mountain educated religious Jews had to scale to accept Jesus as God. He was self-evidently human. They had been taught, over and over again, that God was utterly majestic and powerful, and not visible to human eyes. They had learned the lesson of the exile—to avoid idolatry at all costs. How could they be expected readily to embrace Jesus, a man, as also fully God? It makes it all the more remarkable that any did, and (given this high hurdle they had to climb over to see him for who he was) all the more convincing that Jesus was the true Son of God as he said.

Jesus' answer to the charge of blasphemy has appeared cryptic to many a reader, as it probably did to those who originally heard it. In **verse 34** he quotes from Psalm 82:6—God says, "You are 'gods.'" The point in that psalm is that those who have had these great privileges of not only being made in the image of God but hearing the word of God will be held accountable for how they act and behave just like everyone else, if not more so. "Scripture cannot be set aside," says Jesus (John **10:35**)—that is, this strange text must be true, even though it is unusual, because it is found in the Bible. *So, he says, how can you complain when I, so much more than those who were called "gods" by virtue of their special spiritual advantages, claim to be the Son of God?* It is an argument from the lesser to the greater: *if that is the case, and you accept it, how much more should you not also accept this, which is a far more reasonable thing to claim* (**v 36-37**)?

Why is it a more reasonable thing to claim? Because those spiritually privileged "gods" never did what Jesus has been doing. His "works" prove that he is who he says, and therefore those listening should believe in him (**v 38**). The whole purpose of these works is "that you may know and understand that the Father is in me, and I in the Father." Again they try to grab him, but somehow or other Jesus escapes (**v 39**). His time has not yet come.

The Danger of Familiarity

All the way through this interaction, Jesus is posing the question: *You who are having a Festival of Dedication, will you dedicate yourself to me? Will you express true devotion to God in the midst of your ceremonies of religious devotion?*

Now he moves "across the Jordan," away from the elite "gods" of the temple and the specially religious with their lighted candles at Hanukkah, and back to where John had baptized (**v 40**). This particular trip to the temple had for now come to an end. Ironically, it is here—across the Jordan, and not in the temple at the Festival of Dedication—where people come to believe in him (**v 42**). John the Baptist's work (**v 41**) had prepared the way for people to believe in Jesus. The truth is that, if we are not very careful, familiarity breeds contempt.

Paul's strategy was based upon the observation that those who have not heard will understand, and so his approach was not to build on anyone else's foundation (Romans 15:20). This does not mean that the only acceptable, or fruitful, ministry is pioneer ministry; and nor does this mean that only those who are unfamiliar with the things of the Bible, and are not in attendance at great religious festivals, will understand who Jesus is and have a deep spiritual encounter with him. It does mean that if we are among those who give ourselves to the things of God, and the Scriptures, and religious "institutions" of our day, we must be especially watchful and humble, lest we give in to the typical human tendency to take our relationship with God for granted. Gratitude, thanksgiving, praise, adoration, worship, bowing before Jesus as who he says he is—these prepare the way for us truly and joyfully to encounter God and enjoy life in all its fullness: "He who sacrifices thank offerings honors me, and he prepares the way so that I may show him the salvation of God" (Psalm 50:23, NIV84).

Questions for reflection

1. During which religious festival or season of the year do you find it easiest to forget about Jesus and fail to worship him? What can you do to change how you walk through it?

2. Have you experienced familiarity with "Christian things" breeding contempt or complacency? What can we do to counter this tendency?

3. How will you make sure you memorize, and recall to mind when you need to, verse 28?

11. EATING WITH A DEAD MAN

This section contains some of the most famous words of Jesus because they are often used in funeral services, and appropriately so. But this passage also frees all of us—we mere mortals who, unless Christ first returns, will face death sooner or later—to live life now with the kind of unbridled passion for Christ that can only emerge once we have settled the most significant question of our lives: what will happen to us after we die.

Jesus Does Nothing

As the story begins in **11:1**, we are introduced to Lazarus, who will be the focal point. He lives in Bethany, usually thought to be modern day al-Eizariya, at the home of his sisters, Mary and Martha (**v 2**).

The two sisters send word to Jesus that Lazarus is sick (**v 3**), but Jesus gives his first unexpected response (**v 4**). Given that Jesus had a friendship with this family, we would expect him to hurry along there to comfort, if not heal, the sick man. This, after all, is "the one you love" (**v 3**). Nonetheless, Jesus is unruffled and unperturbed. He knows the plan already: "This sickness will not end in death. No, it is for God's glory so that God's Son may be glorified through it" (**v 4**). There is a purpose to this sickness, which, even if it leads to physical death (as it will), will not end in final death—death in its fullest biblical sense of separation from God. Jesus knows that this sign will show him ("God's Son") as glorious.

The strangest verbal connection is made in **verse 6**: having heard in **verse 5** that Jesus loved this family, we find that John considers it logical that instead of Jesus rushing off to be with Lazarus, he stays where he is somewhat longer. "So when he heard that Lazarus was sick, he stayed where he was two more days." The delay is because of Jesus' love. It is a strange thought that the Lord's love sometimes means delayed answers to the most urgent of requests. Such, though, was the experience of Lazarus and his sisters, and such is the common experience of Christians today. We are not to interpret the Lord's delays as lack of care, but as evidence of love. God's delays very rarely feel loving—understandably enough we want answers to our prayers on a human timescale, and it is hard for us to look at life from the perspective of the One for whom a day is as a thousand years, and a thousand years like a day (2 Peter 3:8). And God does not always give us the reason for his delays, at least not in this life. But we can turn to this story and see that Jesus' delay allowed Lazarus, and everyone there, forevermore to be 100% certain of the resurrection of the dead. Jesus' "delayed" love is a marvelous love.

Death and Life and Death

Jesus' disciples are understandably concerned that they are heading back to Judea, where Jesus' last visit included a narrow escape from execution (John 8:59; 10:31, 39). But, as Jesus points out, they need to learn to make the most of the opportunities for ministry before them: "Are there not twelve hours of daylight? Anyone who walks in the daytime will not stumble, for they see by this world's light" (**11:9**). Each of us has limited moments in this "daytime" to serve God; we all know how hard it is to walk around at night without light, and similarly, without spiritual light we will stumble (**v 10**). How much more precious was each day that was given for the Light of the world to shine?

Then Jesus tells them that Lazarus is only "asleep" and that he is going to "wake him up" (**v 11**). Jesus here means that Lazarus has died, and that he will raise him again, but he uses the phrase "asleep" as a common enough metaphor for physical death with the hope of eternal life. We should not use this text to advance any theory of so-called "soul sleep." When Christians die, we go to be with the Lord (2 Corinthians 5:8), where it is better by far to be (Philippians 1:23). At the end there will be a resurrection of our bodies too (1 Corinthians 15:52; 1 Thessalonians 4:13-18). But, perhaps understandably enough, the disciples misinterpret Jesus to mean that Lazarus is literally asleep (John **11:12**). Once more, the disciples suggest that it might be better if Jesus stays where he is, and they tell Jesus that if Lazarus is asleep, "he will get better" (**v 12**).

John tells us directly what Jesus means, and how the disciples have misunderstood him (**v 13**), and then Jesus himself clarifies his words (**v 14-15**). Lazarus has died, and Jesus is glad he was not there (presumably to heal Lazarus), so that the disciples may believe. Something amazing is about to happen. It is something that Jesus is still glad about, despite Lazarus, whom Jesus loved, being dead. It will explain that his delay was because of his love for Lazarus.

We now come across "doubting Thomas" (**v 16**) in the first of three episodes in John's Gospel that involve him. Already, he appears a little Eeyore-like: "Let us also go, that we may die with him." It is perhaps unfair to dub him "doubting Thomas" when (albeit after some prompting) he became "believing Thomas" (20:28). But the few instances when Thomas appears might lead us to more fairly call him "unenthusiastic Thomas" (14:5; 20:24-28). The reason Thomas speaks about the disciples' own deaths could be related to the geographical location of Bethany, close to Jerusalem (**11:18**); or to the disciples' dawning realization of what it costs to follow Jesus (see 13:37); or (at this stage) Thomas' lack of belief in the possibility of resurrection itself (20:24-28). With a plethora of disciples like that, you would need a cohort of cheerleaders to keep everyone motivated. But for those of us who struggle for enthusiasm and a joyful boldness that embraces costly discipleship rather than seeking to avoid it, it should perhaps be comforting that Jesus' chosen disciples included this sort of character.

Eternity Starts Now

And so Jesus at last sets off for Bethany. Jesus had gone back up to the region where John the Baptist had been baptizing, about 100 miles away (10:40—confusingly, this was the region of Bethany, not the same as the town where Lazarus lived—see 1:28). So the four-day journey down to the Bethany near Jerusalem fits the chronology well (**11:17-18**). Because of the hot climate, bodies were quickly buried, and Lazarus has been dead and in the tomb for four days (**v 17**), so the mourning is in full swing.

The Jews—likely the Jewish leaders again—have come to the home of Martha and Mary to console them (**v 19**). Martha goes to meet Jesus; Mary remains at home (**v 20**). Martha's first words to Jesus are a mixture of complaint, rebuke, and faith (**v 21-22**). What Martha really thinks will happen is now made clear as Jesus tells Martha that Lazarus will rise again (**v 23**). Martha replies that she knows "he will rise again in the resurrection at the last day" (**v 24**). However, Jesus has something much more immediate in mind. The opportunity comes for Jesus to deliver one of his great lines—words which give Christians much courage and boldness in the face of death:

"I am the resurrection and the life. The one who believes in me will live, even though they die; and whoever lives by believing in me will never die." (**v 25-26**)

Jesus is not only saying that he has power over death, though that is true. He is saying that he is the resurrection and the life. To believe in Jesus is to live, for Jesus is life. "Life" in its fullest sense in the Bible, and as used here in John, does not simply mean "existence"; it conveys fullness of life, the life for which we were made and which we can experience in Christ. That life begins when we become a Christian, and though we continue to live physically (and will also die physically as our bodies cease to be alive), our real life is now hidden with Christ in God. In that sense eternal life begins not when we die but when we become a Christian, albeit that that life is interrupted by the painful and horrible realities of our physical death.

A Cambridge professor who was a believing Christian used to do open-air evangelism in the city center. One day he was heckled by a bystander asking him to prove that heaven existed. "My dear fellow," the man replied, "I live there." Even if we physically die, we will live in Jesus (who is life) forever. If Jesus returns first, those who believe in him will never face even physical death (**v 26**; 1 Thessalonians 4:13-18). And wonderfully, Martha believes this, or at least believes as much of it as she is able to grasp (John **11:27**).

She then goes and finds her sister, Mary, and tells her that Jesus is calling for her (**v 28**). Mary, true to form from her reputation in Luke 10:38-42, rushes to see Jesus (John **11:29**). Jesus has not yet come to the village; he is still where Martha met him (**v 30**). The Jews who are consoling the family see Mary leave, assume she is going to the tomb, and follow her (**v 31**).

Mary, once she finds Jesus, falls at his feet. (In worship? In desperation? Probably both.) She says the same as Martha, but without Martha's control and additional statements of faith: "Lord, if you had been here, my brother would not have died" (**v 32**). Jesus, having delayed because he loves them, and not despite his love for them, is now "deeply moved in spirit and troubled" (**v 33**). Many sermons have been preached on the nuances of these words; the point is that Jesus felt, and felt deeply. Whatever it means to be perfectly human, it does not mean an absence of feeling.

> "Jesus wept" says it all when there is nothing else you can say.

Jesus wants to know where Lazarus has been buried (**v 34**). They tell him in the immortal words, "Come and see, Lord." Never was life so poetically bidden to observe death. Now comes the much remarked-upon shortest verse in the Bible: "Jesus wept" (**v 35**). Whoever was responsible for the verse division here struck a shaft of genius: "Jesus wept" says it all when there is nothing else you can say.

The Jews remark on Jesus' love for Lazarus (**v 36**), about which there must have been some doubt, given the delay between Jesus hearing of Lazarus' sickness and traveling to see his stricken (and now deceased) friend. Despite the tears, people conclude that surely if Jesus cared that much, he would have healed Lazarus (**v 37**)? Tears change nothing. But now the answer to the conundrum of Jesus' delay is only just around the corner.

Once more, Jesus is "deeply moved" (**v 38**). Though Jesus is "the resurrection and the life" (**v 25**), death is still in this age a great enemy. Mourning, even weeping, is not an un-Christian thing to do; it is something that Christ did. Yet there can be, and should be, joy as well. Jesus gives the remarkable instruction to pry off the lid of the casket, or "take away the stone" (**v 39**).

Martha—ever-practical Martha—quickly reminds Jesus that four days in a tomb in the Middle East means that there will by now be a considerable stench (**v 39**). But Jesus calls for belief, not for concern: "Did I not tell you that if you believe, you will see the glory of God?" (**v 40**). Jesus then prays, or more accurately gives thanks (**v 41-42**). Why thanksgiving instead of supplication? Some have speculated it was because there was no odor after all when the stone was removed, and so Jesus knew he had been heard. But more likely, Jesus is doing what he says he is doing: giving thanks with confidence that the Father has heard his prayer, so that everyone will know that raising someone from the dead is not hard for him: "I said this for the benefit of the people standing here, that they may believe that you sent me" (**v 42**).

"Jesus called in a loud voice [the volume is presumably for the benefit of those watching] 'Lazarus, come out!'" (**v 43**). The best comment on this verse is still that of Spurgeon: Jesus specifically called Lazarus by name because otherwise, every other dead body would have risen too. Such is the power of him who is the resurrection and the life.

Lazarus comes out—comes out!—still in his grave clothes. Jesus tells those present to unbind him and let him go (**v 44**).

It Would be Best if the Resurrection Died

Unsurprisingly, after seeing a physical resurrection from the dead, quite a few—indeed "many"—believe in him (**v 45**). What is more surprising is that some try to get him into more trouble (**v 46**). What sort of hard heart must you have to see a resurrection and plot a murder? The Pharisees and the Council are now in a quandary. They do not know what to do (**v 47-48**). Their difficulty is not (John now reveals) truly religious, much less spiritual, but political. If everyone believes in Jesus, then their place at the head of the Jewish power structure—which relies on their deal with Rome—will rapidly come under serious threat.

(Some have, of course, wondered how it was that John overhead these words spoken in Council. It could, of course, have been Nicodemus who reported them word for word (3:1; 19:39). Or it could have been John's summary of what we would call the Council minutes. A meeting like this would have been made known, and the basic decision would not be that hard to discover.)

At any rate, the most remarkable part of the discussion is the famous statement by that year's high priest, Caiaphas (**10:49**): "You do not realize that it is better for you that one man die for the people than that the whole nation perish" (**v 50**). John tells us this is prophecy, describing the substitutionary death of Jesus for the Jewish nation and also for all the children of God throughout the world (**v 51-52**). "Prophecy" is an interesting term: Caiaphas is not thereby said to be holy, much less a disciple of Jesus, or even to have been aware that he was making a prophecy, much less cognizant of its full meaning. As a man or woman prophesies, they do so carried along by the Spirit of God, and their words can have greater fulfillments than they themselves can possibly realize. What Caiaphas meant by it was judicial murder (**v 53**); what God meant by it was substitutionary atonement. In God's astonishing sovereign plan, the cross is both (Acts 2:23).

The result of their clearly and openly communicated decision to kill Jesus is that Jesus goes to ground; he no longer walks around "openly," but goes to the "wilderness," to Ephraim, somewhere in the rough country nearby (John **11:54**). It is almost Passover (**v 55**), and they are looking for Jesus, and wondering whether he will put in an appearance at this great feast this time (**v 56**). The result of persecuting the gospel is that you reject the opportunity to hear it; but the gospel still goes forward. The tension is mounting. John's Gospel is moving toward its tragic, glorious climax. The chief priests (**v 57**) are on the lookout and asking for information concerning the whereabouts of this Jesus so that they might—irony of irony—attempt to kill and bury the One who has just gloriously revealed himself to be the resurrection and the life.

Questions for reflection

1. How can this story encourage you when answers to your prayers appear to be delayed?

2. What do Jesus' tears tell you about him, and what difference does it make to how you feel about him today?

3. In what way does the power of Jesus give you strength as you face up to your own mortality?

PART TWO

Eating with friends is surely one of the most pleasant activities in our regular, normal life. When we sit down to a meal, we can find that there is space to talk, converse, and build connections that go beyond the merely mundane. Breaking bread together can build bridges and break down barriers. So throughout the Gospels, whenever we come across Jesus eating with his disciples, we are, if you like, being invited to share a meal with him: to enjoy getting to know, have a relationship with, sup with, and talk with him—to enjoy his company.

It is now "six days before the Passover" (**12:1**). This not only explains why Jesus is once more in the vicinity of Jerusalem in Bethany (presumably at the house of Lazarus, Mary, and Martha), but also indicates that the momentum of his story is gathering pace. The clock is ticking. Six days. Something big is going to happen any time now, John is saying. Jesus' death has been hanging over much (if not all) of the Gospel, but from this point on, that shadow of the cross is becoming clearer and clearer. "Doom went the drums in the deep," as Tolkien put it: six days until Passover. Except it is not doom; it is glory—as Jesus will soon explain (v 12-29). The time is coming. The hour is at hand. Six more days. Each part of the Gospel narrative is leading somewhere, to something—the cross. "We preach Christ crucified," as Paul put it (1 Corinthians 1:23). We live as forgiven people under the banner of the cross, and as commissioned people with the message of the cross.

The Parties and the Perfume

But here, the cross still lies in the near future. Here, it is time to eat. Jesus turns up and they immediately throw a party (John **12:2**). Is this our response to Jesus. If Jesus were to come to our town, would our first thought be, "Quick, let's have a party"? "Go out and buy some steak, put burgers on the grill, invite friends—Jesus is coming." Or would we put on a rather somber religious service—a little bit boring and not too exciting? We are right to approach God with sincere reverence (Hebrews 12:28), but reverence is not the same as stuffiness—the cant and pretention of a form of religion that takes itself seriously while only pretending that it takes God seriously. Heaven, Jesus tells us, is like a banquet, and being with Jesus will be celebration and awe all rolled into one.

Martha, as usual, is serving—though, unlike on the occasion in this home that Luke recounts, she is not rebuked, so presumably she is not grumbling (Luke 10:38-42). The primary importance of learning at Jesus' feet clearly doesn't preclude all background serving of Jesus.

> Learning at Jesus' feet doesn't preclude serving Jesus.

A dinner party like this would take work; Martha is at least doing some of the work and is serving at the table. Lazarus is one of those reclining at the table (John **12:2**). In ancient custom, you did not sit at the table; you reclined. Diners would eat with their right hand, supporting their head on their left and resting on their left elbow, lying in toward the table, and conversing in that manner.

Mary—again perhaps this is characteristic of her passionate devotion—does something that shocked at least one of those present, and which has been ever since a subject of discussion (**v 3**). Milne makes an interesting observation:

> "Mary is mentioned three times in the Gospels and always in association with Jesus' feet ... True service for Jesus springs from a whole-hearted commitment to him as Lord. The feet of Jesus is where service for him begins." (*John*, page 178)

John tells us that what she poured over Jesus was a "pint of pure nard, an expensive perfume" (**v 3**), and it is the expense that sticks in the throat of Judas (**v 4**). This nard, drawn from the plant spikenard found in the foothills of the Himalayas, was famed as an exquisite perfume and would have released an aroma of spicy musk into the air. More to the point, it was a sign of intimacy in the Song of Songs (Song of Songs/Solomon 1:12, ESV). Mary did not hold back: the pint of this expensive perfume that she poured out would have released a strong smell, and the whole house soon caught the whiff of what Mary had done (John **12:3**). Worship of Jesus, in daily life as well as in gathered worship, is to be fulsome and to express the value that Jesus has as the One above all other values: we cannot pinch pennies when it comes to serving God.

Judas, who appears five times in John's Gospel, is a tragic figure. **Verse 5** is the only occasion when John records what Judas actually said, rather than did; it has therefore received considerable attention, not to mention speculation. What he says is that the perfume should have been sold and the money given to the poor (**v 5**). This seems to be, at first glance, a fairly reasonable objection, and so the author, John, immediately explains that the only reason Judas said this was because as the person in charge of the "money bag," he was in the habit of stealing from it for his own purposes: "he was a thief" (**v 6**).

Some have wondered whether Judas' concern for "the poor" displayed a different perspective on Jesus' mission than that of Jesus himself. Could Judas have been part of a more radical group who wished Jesus to have an agenda more focused upon social action—to have a different purpose or priority than dying and saving people spiritually? Such speculation goes beyond the text, and in any case it runs precisely counter to John's own explanation. John tells us the motive: Judas was a thief. He wanted the money from this expensive perfume put in the money bag so that he would have more from which to steal (**v 6**). Those of us in charge of the resources of the kingdom need to take special care to ensure that finances are administered with propriety, both in fact and in appearance. Paul models this dutiful care with the finances of ministries in 2 Corinthians 8:19-21: "We are taking pains to do what is right, not only in the eyes of the Lord but also in the eyes of man."

The main lesson is not, though, merely that taking care of the finances of a ministry puts one in a perilous position (though it does), and should therefore be exercised with systems of accountability in place. The lesson is that people can use apparently moral excuses to do covertly evil things. Judas did not betray Jesus for high-sounding, if utterly misguided, principles; he betrayed him for money. Money scandals only slightly lag behind sex scandals as the most prominent cause of Christian leaders falling from positions of authority, and we would be wise to protect ourselves and others for whom we have responsibility from temptation in both areas.

Even more profoundly, Judas is missing the whole point of Mary's symbolic act. Jesus has come to die. Him seeking to make money out of the saving death of God incarnate proves a thoroughly evil intention.

No Act is Wasted

In John **12:7**, Jesus steps in to protect Mary. Those who do good things for the sake of the gospel often expose themselves to criticism and need leaders to speak up in their defense. Jesus does this: "Leave her alone." His reason, though, for telling Judas to leave her alone is a little more enigmatic, and the translation reflects what is to our ears the ungainly construction: "It was intended that she should save this perfume for the day of my burial." The point seems to be that Mary is to remember what she has just done when it comes to the day of Jesus' death and burial, so that she will be encouraged that this was all forethought and foreordained, and therefore has a purpose. It is possible that she did not use all the perfume, and so, instead of having what was left confiscated to be sold for the poor, Jesus says that she is to keep it and use the rest when Jesus dies—an event that will take place sooner than anyone, apart from Jesus, expects. Even if that was not the case, Mary's action here was not wasted—which is wonderfully encouraging. It is easy for us to think of our acts of service, whether financially or personally costly or both, as amounting to something of little significance in the end. But here is Mary, pouring out a valuable offering to Jesus, and none of it is wasted or inconsequential.

For many of us in the West, time is the most costly item we have to offer: time spent serving Jesus, whether in children's ministries or in the world of business, whether in preaching, or in evangelizing, whether as a leader of a committee or a cleaner of floors. And all of the time we pour out for Jesus as we pour it into serving him is a pleasing aroma to our Lord and Master, and matters now and forever.

Something Worse Than Poverty

Verse 8 has frequently been misinterpreted, and then overcorrected in response, and then misinterpreted again. It is worth remembering that Jesus is replying to an entirely bogus excuse from Judas, who was not really concerned about the poor. It is also clear that part of the role of the New Testament church was to be a place that witnessed to God's love as Christians loved each other so that, as was said of the church after Pentecost, "there were no needy persons among them" (Acts 4:34), in fulfillment of the promise of Deuteronomy 15:4. Yet, while this text should not be used as an excuse for materialism, hoarding of riches, or creating a false dichotomy between caring for "souls" and caring for "bodies," it is a clear indication of a priority, as well as a level-headed description of reality. Jesus apparently does not foresee a time, this side of his return in glory, when the world will be without the poor. That is no reason not to care for the poor, of course. But it is a reason to prioritize the saving work of Christ, which empowers service of the poor and rich alike with the message of the cross: the cross that Jesus prioritized while here. Carson makes a provocative but helpful point:

> "If self-righteous piety sometimes snuffs out genuine compassion, it must also be admitted, with shame, that social activism, even that which meets real needs, sometimes masks a spirit that knows nothing of worship and adoration." (*John*, page 429)

Temporal poverty is a terrible thing; eternal damnation is worse. The gospel empowers and equips us to serve our neighbor and to feed the poor; and the gospel itself is a message of hope for now and also for eternity. That message then is to be prioritized, as Milne points out:

> "The cross must control every aspect of the disciple's life, including alms-giving. Jesus is not presenting us with the competing loyalties of 'spiritual' versus 'material' giving. It is a prime case of both/and, rather than either/or, with each at the proper occasion, and all in the light of the cross." (John, page 177)

The question and challenge for Christ's followers in every age is this: if we are involved in social action and justice missions—and we should be—how can we ensure that service in the name of Christ does not sideline the message of Christ?

Killing Lazarus

Now John takes our gaze away from the inside of the house to the village around it. Jesus is as popular as ever, and a large crowd gathers to see him—but now it is not only Jesus that they want to see, but the one he raised from the dead (John **12:9**). The glory of God is being revealed through Lazarus, just as Jesus said it would be (11:4). The chief priests continue to think that the way to solve their problems is to kill those causing them difficulties (**12:10**)—a solution much resorted to by dictators, despots, and gangsters the world over, but highly inappropriate for chief priests, in addition to being morally repugnant for all. It is also borderline dim: Lazarus has just been raised from the dead. Their solution is to kill him! Perhaps they do not think Jesus could do the same "trick" twice, or that he deceived them last time and it was not a real resurrection. Perhaps they want to demonstrate that Lazarus can die like anyone else, and that Jesus' miracles are no miracles at all. There is a growing desperation to all this, because "many of the Jews were going over to Jesus and believing in him" (**v 11**). What to do? Resist at all costs, and don't by any chance reconsider whether you might just be wrong to oppose a man who can raise the dead.

We should have compassionate pity on those who resist Jesus despite the many opportunities they are given to believe. How terrible will be their fate, unless they are won over and turn and are healed! How awful is the specter of the "chief priests" solemnly strategizing how to kill the Lord of Life. How common it is for people—influential people, authoritative people—to combat the cause of the gospel deliberately and systematically, through what they say, do, and write. Pity them, pray for them, and reach out to them with the gospel, with grace and love and humility and courage. The wealthy and influential are not in need of social-action programs; but they remain desperately in need of the message of the gospel.

We should also be grateful if we do not any more number ourselves among those who oppose Jesus, but instead follow him and worship. It is due to nothing but grace and God's goodness to us. It should cause us to be thankful and full of joy and praise that, through no innate goodness of our own, he has called us to himself. It should cause us to be wary, lest we turn from his teaching and his person to follow after other ways, and, like Judas, miss the life that is before us now. And it should cause us to exuberantly and sacrificially pour out all that we have at his feet, counting not the cost but the privilege of giving what we have to serve him.

Questions for reflection

1. Do you ever treat Jesus' presence in your life as a bothersome nuisance? What would it mean in that moment to change your view of him so that his presence becomes a reason to celebrate with a dinner party?

2. What was it about Jesus' presence that was so deeply attractive to so many people? How can you mirror Jesus' character in your life, through the power of His Spirit?

3. What does it look like for you to love money more than Jesus? How can you guard your heart against the love of money?

12. THE HOUR HAS COME

Leaders often find themselves in the tricky position of discovering that the people they lead do not wish to be led in the direction that it is necessary they go.

There are several possible responses to that situation. One is to say, in the words of the perhaps **apocryphal** quotation attributed to a French Revolutionary leader, "There goes my people; I must follow them, for I am their leader." Leadership becomes an exercise in continuing to be at the front of the "movement"—whichever way the movement is going. Of course, then the leader is no longer really leading; he or she is merely a figurehead, an expression of what the people already want.

The other approach often found in history is some version of dictatorship: *You, the people, will do as I, the leader, want, for fundamentally I know best.* This sort of superior domination is still more common than you might think, even in the West. Many a business is run on the principle of a "benign dictatorship."

Jesus takes neither of those two common approaches. He neither gives in to the wishes of the people and becomes merely a figurehead of a popular movement, nor does he dominate them so that the people become, as it were, merely his underlings, essentially enslaved to his dictatorial will. He takes the third path—the least popular. It's called the way of the cross.

The Treachery of Popularity

Celebrated at churches around the world on "Palm Sunday," this narrative speaks of a King like no other. It begins with a word spreading around the crowd that has gathered in Jerusalem for Passover—Jesus is coming (**v 12**). Are we as excited about the prospect of meeting with Jesus as this crowd—as evidenced by their exuberant shouting—seemed to be? When we congregate in the name of Jesus, we gather to encounter Jesus through his word, by his Spirit. What could be a greater privilege?

The thrill in the crowd prompted them to do what must have seemed extraordinary and frightening to Jesus' opponents. This was a day that would have lived long in the memory of Jesus' disciples. The crowd greets Jesus with clear messianic praise (**v 13**). "Hosanna!" they cry, or "Save [us]!" reflecting the context of Psalm 118, which they obviously know well: "LORD, save us! LORD, grant us success!" (Psalm 118:25). The branches which they wave in celebration are also mentioned in that psalm: "The LORD is God, and he has made his light shine on us. With boughs in hand, join in the festal procession up to the horns of the altar" (v 27).

This is turning into a day of astonishing celebration, worship, and adulation of Jesus as King-Messiah. As has often been noted, this praise will not last, as was expressed in the words of Samuel Crossman's hymn written in 1664:

Sometimes they strew his way,
And his sweet praises sing;
Resounding all the day
Hosannas to their King:
Then "Crucify!"
is all their breath,
And for his death
they thirst and cry.

Some have said that this is not strictly accurate, or at least not certainly so: there is no explicit mention that the same people who sang Jesus' praise here were those who later shouted, "Crucify!" (though there is no indication that they were not). But regardless, this is fiddling with poetic license in a rather literalistic way. The point Crossman (and preachers before and after him) is seeking to make is that the city that first welcomed Jesus with open arms soon crucified him:

> "On a human level, the public acclaim for Jesus, which turns into a mob calling, 'Crucify him!'… in a matter of days, highlights the treacherous nature of popularity. Theologically, the triumphal entry is shown to fulfill OT prophecy. Because palm branches commonly were used to convey the celebration of victory, the image of Jesus here is that of a victor who has defeated his enemies." (Köstenberger, *John,* page 367)

It is easy for those of us who follow Jesus to sing his sweet praises when the atmosphere is right, the mood hits us, or we are surrounded by others who support the same idea, intention, and value system as our own. But what about when we are faced with opponents of Christ? Will we stand tall then? To be able to follow Jesus consistently, even in the face of adversity demands more than simply a brief emotional sing-song; it requires a heartfelt commitment that is rooted in the redeeming and sanctifying work of the Spirit of Jesus within that heart. The disciples who turned tail at Calvary preached passionately at Pentecost—because the Spirit of Jesus clothed them with his power of grace and humility, faith and love, truth and perseverance even in face of adversity. The Spirit's work gives us the ability to stand tall for Jesus every day; and it removes any excuse for not doing so.

Donkey King

Famously, Jesus rides into Jerusalem on a donkey (John **12:14**). John tells us that this is in fulfillment of the prophecy found in Zechariah 9:9: "Do not be afraid, Daughter Zion; see, your king is coming, seated on a donkey's colt" (John **12:15**). This symbolism would have been apparent to all who observed it: donkeys are not warhorses. Zechariah himself makes the metaphor explicit. The king would be "lowly and riding on a donkey … I will take away the chariots from Ephraim and the warhorses from Jerusalem, and the battle bow will be broken. He will proclaim peace to the nations. His rule will extend from sea to sea and from the River to the ends of the earth" (Zechariah 9:9-10). This humble king is a model to all leaders; we lead as those who serve. We who lead others must first serve others; we must first be led by the King if we wish to be a leader in our communities, our churches, our families, or anywhere else.

> We who lead others must first serve others.

Jesus' disciples cannot help but to be caught up in the mood of this moment, as in a carnival or a citywide celebration of a sporting triumph. Yet they do not really grasp the point (John **12:16**). They see the branches; they hear the praise; they observe the donkey. Later, they will interpret all this as related to Jesus being a crucified, glorified King. For now, they just enjoy the smiles and cheers. The crowd, meanwhile, is still high on the miraculous sign of Lazarus being raised from the dead (**v 17**). They are telling everyone who will listen about it. Wouldn't you? It is this "sign" that now drives their attention to Jesus (**v 18**). And in another unconscious prophecy, the Pharisees shake their heads at each other and commiserate with one another over how their plots are coming to nothing: "Look how the whole world has gone after him!" (**v 19**).

It has indeed, and John next picks up on this unintended prophecy by giving a remarkable example of its fruition. Some Greeks are in town too, and they want to see Jesus (**v 20**). The "world" (**v 19**)—the nations—is coming to Jesus, the significance of which Leon Morris explains:

> "[Jesus] no longer belongs to Judaism, which in any case has rejected him. But the world, whose Savior he is, awaits him and seeks for him." (The Gospel According to John, page 524)

The magnetic pull of the Christ is drawing in disciples from outside of the narrow confines of pharisaically-defined rabbinic Judaism.

When we exalt the cross of Christ, we find that others of all nations, creeds, and kinds are drawn to him too. With our eyes on Christ, the barriers that threaten to divide us—be they ones of race, culture, tribe or generation—fade into insignificance, and Jew and Gentile worship at his feet.

Philip and Andrew are once again examples to us of eager excitement about the growing kingdom of the Messiah (**v 21-22**—see 1:41-45). Jesus at once sees the significance of what they tell him about these Greeks: "The hour has come for the Son of Man to be glorified" (**12:23**). This is key. John is beginning to move in his Gospel from the "book of signs" to the "book of glory," and this is an indication of that coming structural change, which begins at the start of chapter 13:

> "The raising of Lazarus, the anointing at Bethany, and Jesus' triumphal entry into Jerusalem mark a transition from Jesus' public ministry to the Jews to his private ministry to his disciples and his passion." (Köstenberger, *John,* page 374)

Dying to Live

In one of those magisterial principles uttered by our Master, Jesus turns his own example into an eternal lesson couched in the most homely of metaphors. Who could listen to this man speak and not wonder whether he was more than a man? "Very truly," Jesus begins, in his characteristic way of drawing attention to a key saying, "I tell you, unless a kernel of wheat falls to the ground and dies, it remains only a single seed. But if it dies, it produces many seeds" (**12:24**). Like a seed that is sown, apparently dead, and then springs up alive after having been put in the ground, so Jesus will be "sown" into the ground, and through his death and resurrection there will come much global fruit. The way to be fruitful is to die.

We too, Jesus teaches, are to die to ourselves in order to bear fruit for him. Jesus' life and death save us, but they are also an example to us: "Anyone who loves their life will lose it, while anyone who hates their life in this world will keep it for eternal life" (**v 25**). There is an inevitable conflict: we cannot "love our life"—that is, we cannot want what we want selfishly, for ourselves—and expect that way of life to give us true life. The human condition is such that our "selves," though we were made to find life in worshipful obedience of God, are now set on a self-absorbed trajectory. Only as we die to our selfish selves can we find life as we were meant to enjoy it, in fellowship with God. We must die to ourselves to live to Christ and to find real life in him.

In case anyone finds this too high a calling, Jesus quickly reassures: we are following Jesus and the pattern he has set (**v 26**), and like Jesus we will rise again to new life. (The disciples would surely look back on these words and remember them when they faced their own deaths.) Plus, Jesus adds, the Father honors those who serve his Son. It is a saying that appears to reflect the thinking of the second part of 1 Samuel 2:30. What great motivation there is here, freely given by Jesus, to serve him! The Father bestows true honor on those who serve Jesus. In the strange economy of God, service leads to honor and death leads to life, while self-preservation leads only to destruction.

A Voice From Heaven

But this path is not an easy one to walk. Even Jesus cannot but be "troubled" by the prospect of his coming death (John **12:27**). He wonders aloud whether he should ask the Father God to keep him from his "hour"—that is, his crucifixion. But some prayers are best left unprayed, when we can discern God's purpose. So instead Jesus chooses to pray, "Father, glorify your name"—a prayer that is safe to utter at any time. In confirmation of the extraordinary holiness which that decision reveals, a voice speaks from heaven: "I have glorified it, and will glorify it again" (**v 28**). Jesus' name is glorious from eternity, and it will be shown as such at his death and resurrection.

This "voice" from heaven was clearly audible: the crowd heard the voice too (**v 29**). Some "said it had thundered." What John means by drawing attention to the crowd's description of the thunderous quality of the voice is not crystal clear, but it is likely echoing an appearance of God—a theophany—at Sinai, in Exodus 19:16. Similarly, the explanation "an angel had spoken to him" (John **12:29**) seems to refer to Sinai (tradition held that the giving of the law at Sinai involved angelic ministry in some way—see Galatians 3:19). The people around Jesus realize that somehow in the voice from heaven, and in the presence of Jesus, they are in the presence of the divine. Certainly John wants us to realize that this is God incarnate.

Jesus himself gives an interpretation of the voice (John **12:30**). It was a witness "for your benefit," because this is now a supremely important moment. "Now is the time for judgment on this world" (**v 31**). He is not referring here to the final judgment, but to the judgment upon which that final judgment will take place, and upon which they will stand at the final judgment. That judgment—God's positive judgment on his Son as he raises him up—will be given at the cross, and so he will draw people from all nations to himself. His standard is the standard by which all will be judged now and forever (see **v 48**)—and this is a standard we cannot meet but can only be given, by faith. Indeed, "the prince of this world" (a description of the one who deserves no **appellation**, the devil) will be defeated (**v 31**). While he will still keep on fighting in vain, the cross will be God's victory over the forces of darkness by drawing all people to Christ through the counter-intuitive, sacrificial power of the cross. When Jesus is "lifted up," he will draw all people to himself (**v 32**). In this verse there is a great principle of mission, and therefore of racial reconciliation. As Jesus is lifted up at the cross, Jesus will be able to draw people from all nations to himself.

The crowd understands, as John explains to us in **verse 33**, that this is somehow referring to Jesus' death. They are still thinking about "the Law" (**v 34**—likely, John means the Old Testament Scriptures)— and realize that the Messiah's kingdom is an eternal kingdom. What they do not realize is the centrality of the suffering of the Messiah. In particular, they remain uncertain as to the identity of the divine-human figure from Daniel's prophecy: "the Son of Man" (Daniel 7:13-14).

Jesus replies by returning to one of his (and John's) favorite metaphors, that of light: "You are going to have the light just a little while longer. Walk while you have the light, before darkness overtakes you" (John **12:35**). Jesus is the light, as he has already said. His identity as the God-Man could not have been made clearer through his words and works. These people have an opportunity now to believe in him, the "light," and Jesus wants them to make the most of it: "Believe in the light while you have the light [that is, Jesus], so that you may become children of light" (**v 36**). Here is a warning to us all: we must make the most of the word of Christ as we receive it now. It is as we believe it that we are transformed by it increasingly into his likeness, as "children of light."

Questions for reflection

1. What gets in the way of you praising Jesus exuberantly? How would reflecting on Jesus' identity as your Savior ("Hosanna!"), and as your powerful-yet-humble King ("seated on a donkey's colt"), help provoke your praise?

2. How could you use Psalm 118 as a way of personally reminding yourself of the goodness of Jesus?

3. Jesus' teaching about dying to self is meant to be challenging, and to change us. In what ways do you need to apply this to your own life?

PART TWO

Contemporary ministry and Christian living are often presented as one victory after another—and when there is a failure, it is seen as an aberration. This is not what we find in this section of John's Gospel!

Certainly, we are to foster cultures, programs, teaching and discipleship that are most likely to lead to effective ministry and outreach. But part of the reality of this world is that we will at times be faced with the truth that not everyone will "get it." There are those who do not, and will not, "believe" (**v 37**), however much we try to persuade them. It could be someone in a ministry situation; it could be a family member; it could be a friend or a colleague. We can see from the pages of the Bible, not least in this Gospel, that by no means did everyone accept Jesus' message. Humanly speaking, that is why he died. This reality does not discourage us; it gives us ballast, grit, and—paradoxically—confidence.

By no means are we to seek rejection, or to live the Christian life in such a way that it looks unattractive. Quite the reverse: we are to commend Christ to family, friends and co-workers. But, in the end, it is also the case that not all will accept the Christ we commend. And that (hard) truth gives perseverance to wobbly saints who faint at the first sign of a lack of faith from others.

John indicates the closing of this section of his narrative in **verse 37**: even though Jesus had done all these signs, "they still would not believe in him." It must have been frustrating for him. But it should reassure us when we are active in ministry—sometimes in impressive or even miraculous ministry—and yet we do not see the impact that we had hoped for and prayed for. If God incarnate can perform miracles and "they still would not believe in him," we can be consoled when one of our better sermons or evangelistic discussions falls flat. And we should also be warned against equating attendance at or involvement in exciting ministry with genuine faith. If it is possible to see Jesus himself perform miracles in front of you and yet still not have authentic faith, then it is certainly possible to attend a solid Bible-teaching church and still lack faith. Christ is not looking for mere theoretical devotion or acknowledgement of his power; he wants actual commitment, true trust, a personal engagement and investment in him at the most practical of levels. And that often keeps the numbers down.

Deeper Blindness

In this particular case, the unbelief is a specific fulfillment of a prophetic trajectory from the Old Testament, in particular from Isaiah. "Lord, who has believed our message and to whom has the arm of the Lord been revealed?" (**v 38**, quoting Isaiah 53:1). When Isaiah wrote those words, he presumably did not know anything of John **12:38**, and his original hearers and readers certainly did not. Yet his words find their final fulfillment at this moment: Jesus, as the fulfillment of the whole prophetic ministry, also fulfills what happens to prophets themselves, even those whose words were backed up by miracles: rejection (**v 39**).

What could account for such a remarkable inability to see who Jesus was from what he had done and said? There is only one possible explanation, John shows, again quoting from the prophet Isaiah (**v 40**, Isaiah 6:10). Blindness. Hardness. There is no fault in Jesus; there is no lack of evidence. The fault is in us, in humanity; for by nature we cannot see, and will not believe, because we are blind of eye and hard of heart. As Calvin put it:

> "There is nothing less reasonable than that truth should not differ from falsehood, that the bread of life should become a death-dealing poison and that medicine should make a disease worse. But men's malice is to blame, which turns life into death."
>
> (*Calvin's New Testament Commentaries,* Vol. 1, page 47)

The human heart is not naturally good and not liable to believe the good; it is naturally wicked and liable to be suspicious of what is right and beautiful. On our **doctrines** of humanity and of sin hang so much of how we live, and how we react to others. Do we consider the central problem as being that humans are deprived, and require education in order to thrive; or that humans are depraved, and require gospel evangelism, followed by gospel education, in order to grow and become all that they were made to be? According to the Bible, we naturally have blind spiritual eyes, and need the sovereign work of God to enlighten those eyes. A person's rejection of truth leads to a further inability to be able to receive it; shutting the eyes against the truth in the end so paralyzes spiritual sight that a person cannot open their eyes to that truth.

Having quoted from Isaiah, John now explains how it is possible that the prophet could have been talking about Jesus. He may not have known about the specific circumstances of the second half of John 12, but he was thinking about Jesus. In fact, he saw Jesus: "Isaiah said this because he saw Jesus' glory and spoke about him" (John **12:41**). Isaiah, perhaps in his encounter with "the Lord, high and exalted" in Isaiah 6, saw the glorious Son of God before his incarnation. And having seen him, he spoke of him. His whole ministry was directed toward him.

Despite the general rejection of Jesus by those who had seen the signs, there was nonetheless a wider reception of him and his ministry, even by those among "the leaders" (John **12:42**). Many did believe in him. We should not be like Elijah, despairing that only he had not bowed the knee before Baal (1 Kings 19:14-18). We are part of the church, and there are always others who are faithfully following Jesus. There are those who have gone before us, those who are around us, and those who will come after us. Here in John 12 there is a remnant—a shoot from a dry branch—that still emerge into some sort of faith.

Glory-Hunting

But it is not the kind of faith that is willing to suffer. Even the best of us can quail when faced with opposition, and the faith in these people is not yet the faith that will allow them to face persecution for

Christ. Their problem is a fear of the Pharisees, who may throw them out of the synagogue (John **12:42**). They have learnt this lesson from the man born blind: *Do not confess Jesus or you will be expelled from the community* (9:22, 34). And they are not willing to bear that cost, because "they [love] the glory that comes from man more than the glory that comes from God" (**12:43**, ESV).

Whatever stage of the Christian life we are at, we must beware, lest we fall into the same trap. Whose glory is it that we seek? That of people—or that of the Other? The glory and approval of people is infinitely disappointing and ultimately murderous; it is far less satisfying than the all-surpassing glory of the Eternal One. To hear one word of praise from him is worth more than a lifetime of approval from this world.

Glory is going to be a key concept from here on in John's Gospel—a decisive criterion, a divider between those who follow Jesus and those who retreat before the disapproval of others. In the end, we all must make the same choice: are we seeking man's glory or God's; man's definition of greatness or God's; man's praise and approval or God's; man's standard of success or God's? There may be times when a lack of opposition and a comfortable life hide the clarity and necessity of this choice; but in the end we will all have to decide whose approval we would rather have: that of Jesus, or that of other people.

In response to this faltering faith, which quaked at the prospect of losing human praise, Jesus "cried out, 'Whoever believes in me does not believe in me only, but in the one who sent me'" (**v 44**). Faith in Jesus is the standard by which we can tell whether someone is seeking God's glory or not. If you reject Jesus, it is because you reject God, since Jesus is the perfect revelation of God himself (**v 45**). What a countercultural statement in today's politically correct, multi-religious world!

Now and the Future

In **verse 46**, Jesus once more returns to one of the key themes in John's Gospel—"light." This salvation that he is bringing is going to be like bringing people who are in darkness out into the light. It is evocative imagery, often repeated in John. Sin is like darkness: you cannot see; you stumble. Salvation is like coming into the light: all is clear now. When you turn the lights on, it is always surprising to see what is left in the dark corners of a room that has not been dusted for months. The light of Christ shines into the nooks and crannies of our lives, to show us where we need to be cleaned up and bring our lives more into line with his character through the power of the gospel.

> Salvation is like coming into the light: all is clear now.

In **verse 47**, Jesus indicates that the judgment which he would bring would not take place at that time. Jesus will judge (5:22; see also 2 Timothy 4:1), but his ministry in his first coming was not one of judgment, but of salvation. Nonetheless, his point here is even more acute: Jesus is saying that the words that he speaks during his first coming will judge those who reject him on the last day, on the occasion of his second coming (John **12:48**). How we have responded to Jesus' words will be the basis of his final judgment—and, in the context of **verses 42-43**, the challenge seems to be not whether we accept Jesus' teaching privately, but whether we live it publically, as Milne states:

"Those who expect the Lord to own their names on judgment day, he expects to own his name now before a watching world. There is no such thing as a totally secret disciple."

(*John*, page 194)

Sometimes, in extremity, it is good to remember that there is this motivation to be faithful unto death: then we shall bear the crown of life. When faced with criticism, trial or persecution, remember that you are living for an eternal judgment that will far outlast mere temporal trials, however terrible they may currently appear.

Life to the Full, Life Forever

Verse 49 is one of those verses that might trouble someone with a simplistic understanding of the Trinity, but grasping its meaning involves no more than seeing that the Trinity is a relationship of voluntary submission, and that such submission does not require a diminishing of status. In the Trinity, the Father sends and Jesus goes, but they are both fully God. It is a model of how we are to relate to each other, submitting to one another out of reverence for Christ (Ephesians 5:21). This is what the Son is doing: "For I did not speak on my own, but the Father who sent me commanded me to say all that I have spoken" (John **12:49**). In the eternal relationship of the triune God, Father, Son and Holy Spirit exist in perfect union and yet also with distinct roles. Jesus touches on this mystery here. It has a practical application: following someone else's authority does not diminish your essential status as equal to them (otherwise this verse would diminish Jesus' deity). In Christ's view, authority is an exercise of service, not of domination, and submission is an exercise of love, not of self-mutilation.

Verse 50 closes this section with a note of finality and the hope of "eternal life." Jesus is speaking as the Father has commanded, and this command leads us to life forever—life with Jesus through believing in him and in his word.

The command here anticipates the "new commandment" that is coming (13:34; 14:15, 21; 15:10, 12, 14, 17), and that we will look at in the second volume of this guide to John's Gospel. It also rounds off this section of the Gospel, and this first volume, with a reminder that the command of God the Father, as spoken by God the Son, Jesus, is the word that gives life. This life that comes through faith in Jesus and his word is not merely existence, or even existence extended eternally. It is life in its fullest sense, life abundant, life "to the full" (10:10).

This life is to be found "in him": "In him was life, and that life was the light of all mankind" (1:4). We experience this "life" through receiving him, and enjoying relationship with God through and alongside Jesus: "To all who did receive him, to those who believed in his name, he gave the right to become children of God" (1:12). We are in this family, sharing his life, because though "no one has ever seen

God … the one and only Son, who is himself God and is in closest relationship with the Father, has made him known" (1:18).

John has shown us the Word, the Son of God, our Lord Jesus, walking, speaking and doing signs so that those who met him then and meet him today might believe. We have seen that some have met him and believed, albeit in seed form; and as we turn the corner of this Gospel from the book of signs to the book of glory—as we move toward the place where the Son of Man will be glorified at the cross— we are called, like John's first readers, to find our life in him, through faith in him, by receiving his word. *The thief has come to steal and kill and destroy,* Jesus says to us. *But I have come that you might have life, and life to the full.* Receive him, follow him, love, obey and enjoy him—and find life in him today.

Questions for reflection

1. It is astonishing to realize that after all Jesus' miraculous brilliance, he was still rejected. How can this encourage us to keep on going in our witness, despite lack of apparent success?

2. How do you find yourself seeking glory that comes from others? How does 12:42-43 help us spot that? And how would you behave differently if God's glory was paramount in your mind and heart?

3. If you had to sum up the Jesus you meet in the first twelve chapters of John's Gospel in five words, what would they be?

GLOSSARY

Abraham: (also called Abram) the ancestor of the nation of Israel, and the man God made a binding agreement (covenant) with. God promised to make his family into a great nation, give them a land, and bring blessing to all nations through one of his descendants (see Genesis 12:1-3).

Acronym: where each letter in an abbreviation stands for a word, e.g. NASA = the National Aeronautics and Space Administration.

Affectional: driven by the inclinations of our hearts. Our affections are what drive and shape our emotions.

Analogy: a comparison between two things, usually using one of them to explain or clarify the other.

Anarthrous: grammatical term, meaning that the original Greek word does not have an article (a short word that goes before a noun, e.g. the, a, an). So in John 1:1, for instance, the literal Greek translation would be "and God was Word."

Anti-type: the opposite.

Aphorisms: memorable sayings that contain truth.

Apocryphal: probably made up, fictional.

Apologetic: a reasoned argument to defend the Christian faith.

Apostle: a man appointed directly by the risen Christ to teach about him with authority.

Appellation: title.

Archetype: best example.

Ascension: when Jesus left earth to return to heaven, to sit and rule at God the Father's right hand (see Acts 1:6-11; Philippians 2:8-11).

Begotten: a word traditionally used to capture something of the order of the three Persons of the Trinity. Father, Son, and Spirit are all eternal (i.e. never created). By saying that the Son is "begotten" of the Father, we mean that the Father is the first person of the Trinity and the Son the second (the Spirit is the third). Father, Son, and Spirit are equal in deity and different in role.

Blasphemous: when God is disrespected or mocked, or conduct or speech that will cause God to be disrespected or mocked.

Canon: the collection of texts which are accepted as God's word.

Caviling: petty and unnecessary.

Chauvinistic: aggressively prejudiced (usually refers to prejudice against women).

Church father: prominent Christian theologians from the first few centuries of the life of the church.

Circular reasoning: a line of argument that begins with the conclusion, e.g. "A is true because B is true; B is true because A is true."

Commentators: people who write books studying (or, more broadly, who offer opinions regarding) biblical texts.

Commissions: gives a specific responsibility, appointment, or job.

Corollary: an argument that follows on.

David: the second king of Israel, whose reign was the high point of Israel's history. God promised that one of David's descendants would reign forever—the Messiah (see 2 Samuel 7). The **Davidic kingdom** refers to the reign of this promised king.

Depravity: natural corruptness and sinfulness.

Doctrine: the study of what is true about God and what he has revealed.

Doubting Thomas: a common way of describing the disciple who refused to believe that Jesus had been resurrected until he saw the risen Lord for himself (see John 20:24-29).

Elect: those to whom God has chosen to give saving faith, so that they become Christians. The truth that only those who are chosen by God will be saved is known as the doctrine of **election**.

Epilogue: a book's conclusion or the author's closing comment.

Epistemological: relating to epistemology, which is the theory of knowledge and the study of how we distinguish between justifiable, reasonable belief and mere opinion.

Evangelical: Christians who emphasize the Bible's authority and the need to be personally converted through faith in Jesus' death and resurrection.

Evangelical Awakening: period during the 1730s and 1740s when powerful preaching "awakened" thousands of people in Protestant Europe and the American colonies to the truth of evangelical beliefs (see definition above).

Evocative: bringing strong images and feelings to mind.

Exegesis: the study of a text, seeking to understand what it meant in the context in which it was first written and/or heard.

Exposition: explanation of a text.

Fait accompli: something that has already happened or been decided, so that those hearing of it have no choice but to accept it. From the French for "accomplished fact."

False dichotomy: an unnecessary division between two things.

Fatalistic: believing that everything is impersonally predetermined and therefore inevitable; we make no real decisions.

Grace: unmerited favor. In the Bible, "grace" is usually used to describe how God treats his people. Because God is full of grace, he gives believers eternal life (Ephesians 2:4-8); he also gives them gifts to use to serve his people (Ephesians 4:7, 11-13).

Half-caste: an offensive term for someone who is mixed-race.

Heretics: people who, despite being challenged, continue to hold to a belief which directly opposes Scripture.

High-church: theology and church worship that focus on ritual; influenced by Roman Catholicism.

Host: term used in some churches for the bread blessed during Holy Communion.

Human condition: the things that are a fundamental and universal part of being human. In the Christian view, part of the "human condition" is that all people are under the effect of sin.

Incarnation: the coming of the divine Son of God as a human, in the person of Jesus of Nazareth.

Incipiently: beginning; developing.

Irony: a mismatch (often humorous, sometimes tragic) between what is expected and what actually is.

Isaac: the promised son of Abraham. God tested Abraham by asking him to sacrifice Isaac, but intervened to stop him from doing so at the last moment. God provided a ram for the sacrifice instead (see Genesis 22).

Jehovah's Witnesses: a religious organization which shares some doctrines with Christianity, but which (among other major differences) denies the Trinity.

Job: an Old Testament character who endured great suffering as a test of his faith. **Job's "comforters"** were friends who encouraged him to curse God for his circumstances, but Job rightly refused.

Johannine scholar: someone who studies the Gospel of John.

Jonathan Edwards: preacher and writer (1703 – 1758), and a key figure in the Evangelical Awakening (see above).

King Herod: the ruler of much of Israel at the time of Jesus' adult ministry (one of several related King Herods mentioned in the New Testament).

Kosher: food that satisfied the requirements of the Old Testament food laws. Also now a slang term for "legitimate."

Legalism: a way of living that obeys certain rules in the belief that keeping these requirements will earn some form of blessing (for example, eternal life or worldly wealth).

Literary: referring here to John's Gospel as a respected piece of literature on the basis of the quality of its writing.

Lot: Abraham's nephew, who was rescued by angels from the destruction of the wicked city of Sodom (Genesis 19).

Low church: the opposite of **high church** (see definition above).

Manna: the "bread" that God miraculously provided each morning for the Israelites to eat while they were journeying to the promised land (see Exodus 16). It looked like white flakes.

Messiah: Christ, the anointed one. In the Old Testament, God promised that the Messiah would come to rescue and rule his people. Jesus' **messianic signs** (miracles) proved that he was indeed the Messiah.

Metaphor: images which are used to explain something, but that are not to be taken literally (e.g. "The news was a dagger to his heart").

Monotheistic: believing that there is only one ("mono") God.

Motif: recurring idea or pattern.

Nefarious: wicked; wrong.

New covenant: a covenant is a binding agreement or promise. The old covenant set out how believers in the Old Testament related to God; Jesus established the new covenant, so believers now relate to God through Jesus' saving death and resurrection.

Oral: designed to be spoken out loud.

Parable: a memorable story that illustrates a truth about Jesus and/ or his kingdom.

Pariah: social outcast.

Passion: the events of the week leading up to and including Jesus' death, from his entrance into Jerusalem to his crucifixion.

Pastoral ministry: the work of shepherding and caring for God's people, primarily by teaching from the Bible.

Pentecostal/charismatic: used here as a very general term describing churches which emphasize the work of the Holy Spirit in Christian life and worship and the continuation of all of the Spirit-given abilities and gifts listed out in the New Testament.

Perseverance: continuing to do or believe something in the face of difficulty. The doctrine of "perseverance of the saints" teaches that true Christians will never fall away from the faith (sometimes expressed as "once saved, always saved").

Pharisaism: the Pharisees were leaders of a first-century Jewish sect who were extremely strict about keeping God's laws, and who added extra laws around God's law to ensure that they wouldn't break it. They tended to focus on external acts of obedience. Today this word has a meaning similar to **legalism** (see definition above).

Pilate: the Roman governor who oversaw the trial and execution of Jesus under Roman law.

Pre-existent: existing from an earlier time.

Prologue: the introduction to a piece of writing.

Promised land: the land on the eastern coast of the Mediterranean Sea that God promised Abraham he would give his descendants (Genesis 12:6-8; 13:14-18).

Providence: the way that God chooses to work in the world.

Puritans: members of a sixteenth and seventeenth-century movement in Great Britain which was committed to the Bible as God's word, to simpler worship services, to greater commitment and devotion to following Christ, and increasingly to resisting the institutional church's hierarchical structures. Many emigrated to what would become the US, and were a strong influence on the church in many early colonies.

Rabbi: a Jewish religious teacher.

Redemption: the act of redeeming, or releasing, sinners. By dying on the cross, Jesus paid the penalty for sin to release Christians from slavery to sin, death, and judgment (see Romans 3:23-25; Ephesians 1:7).

Reformer: one of the first two generations of people in the sixteenth and early-seventeenth centuries who preached the gospel of justification by faith, and opposed the Pope and the Roman church (a period of history known as the **Reformation**).

Relativistically: related to relativism—the idea that there is no absolute right and wrong. Instead, right and wrong change, depending on one's situation, culture, and/or experience. So something can be wrong for you, but right for me.

Rhetoric: persuasive writing.

Salacious: obsessed with sex.

Salvific: relating to salvation (being saved from sin).

Samaritan: people from the region of Samaria; a people group with mixed Jewish-pagan ancestry and religion.

Sanctified: made holy.

Serial monogamy: a series of sexual relationships with one partner after another.

Soul sleep: the erroneous view that after death a person's soul "sleeps" until the dead are raised on the day of judgment.

Sovereignty: supreme authority / being the supreme ruler.

Syncretists: people who incorporate aspects of different religions into their beliefs; seeking to combine religions into one system of belief.

Systematic theology: an approach to theology (the study of what is true about God) that seeks to gather and organize all that the Bible says on a particular area of doctrine.

Temporal: material (as opposed to spiritual).

Theological treatises: academic books on the subject of theology (the study of what is true about God).

Torah: the five books of Moses in the Jewish Scriptures (i.e. Genesis, Exodus, Leviticus, Numbers, and Deuteronomy).

Trinitarianism: the biblical doctrine that the one God is three Persons, distinct from one another, each fully God, of the same "essence" (or "God-ness"). We usually call these three Persons Father, Son, and Holy Spirit.

Veracity: accuracy.

Works-righteousness: the belief that a person's works (i.e. thoughts, words, and actions) can bring them into right relationship with God.

Worldview: the beliefs we hold in an attempt to make sense of the world as we experience it, and which direct how we live in it. Everyone has a worldview.

BIBLIOGRAPHY

■ C.K. Barrett, *Essays on John* (Westminster Press, 1982)

■ F.F. Bruce, *The Gospel of John* (Eerdmans, 1983)

■ John Calvin, *Calvin's New Testament Commentaries,* Vol. 1 (Eerdmans, 1971)

■ D.A. Carson, *John* in The Pillar New Testament Commentary series (IVP UK, 1992)

■ Jonathan Edwards, *Thoughts on the New England Revival,* Vol. 1 (Banner of Truth, 2005)

■ Ed. Joel C. Elowsky, *Ancient Christian Commentary on Scripture, New Testament IVa,* (IVP Academic, 2007)

■ S. Hamid-Khani, *Revelation and Concealment of Christ: A Theological Inquiry into the Elusive Language of the Fourth Gospel* in the Wissenschaftliche Untersuchungen Zum Neuen Testament 2. Reihe series (Mohr Siebeck, 2000)

■ Matthew Henry, Commentary on the Whole Bible, accessible online at ccel.org/ccel/henry

■ Andreas J. Köstenberger, *John* in the Baker Exegetical Commentary on the New Testament series (Baker Academic, 2004)

■ Bruce Milne, *John* in the Bible Speaks Today series (IVP USA, 1993)

■ Leon Morris, *The Gospel According to John* in the New International Commentary on the New Testament series (Eerdmans, 1995)

■ J.O.F. Murray, *Jesus According to S. John* (Longmans, Green & Co., 1936)

■ J.C. Ryle, *Expository Thoughts on the Gospel of John* (Banner of Truth, 1987)

■ C.H. Spurgeon, *The Metropolitan Tabernacle Pulpit Original and Completely Unabridged Sermons Preached and Revised* (Pilgrim Publications, 1995)

■ P.J. Williams, "Not the Prologue of John" in the *Journal for the Study of the New Testament* (2011)

John for...
Bible-study Groups

Josh Moody's **Good Book Guide** to John 1–12 is the
companion to this resource, helping groups of Christians
to explore, discuss and apply John's Gospel together.
Eight studies, each including investigation, apply, getting
personal, pray and explore more sections, take you
through the first half of the Gospel. Includes a concise
Leader's Guide at the back.

Find out more at:
www.thegoodbook.com/goodbookguides

Daily Devotionals

Explore daily devotional helps you open up the Scriptures and will encourage and equip you in your walk with God. Published as a quarterly booklet, *Explore* is also available as an app, where you can download notes on John, alongside contributions from trusted Bible teachers including Timothy Keller, Mark Dever, Juan Sanchez, Tim Chester and Sam Allberry.

Find out more at:
www.thegoodbook.com/explore

More For You

1 Samuel For You

"As we read this gripping part of Israel's history, we see Jesus Christ with fresh color and texture. And we see what it means for his people to follow him as King in an age that worships personal freedom."

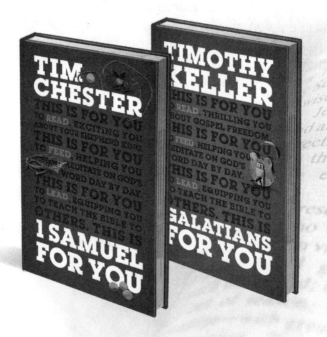

Galatians For You

"The book of Galatians is dynamite. It is an explosion of joy and freedom which leaves us enjoying a deep significance, security and satisfaction. Why? Because it brings us face to face with the gospel—the A to Z of the Christian life."

The Series

John 1–12 For You is the fifteenth in the *God's Word For You* series. Other titles are:

- **Exodus For You** *Tim Chester*
- **Judges For You** *Timothy Keller*
- **1 Samuel For You** *Tim Chester*
- **Daniel For You** *David Helm*
- **Luke 1-12 For You** *Mike McKinley*
- **Luke 12-24 For You** *Mike McKinley*
- **Romans 1-7 For You** *Timothy Keller*
- **Romans 8-16 For You** *Timothy Keller*
- **Galatians For You** *Timothy Keller*
- **Ephesians For You** *Richard Coekin*
- **Philippians For You** *Steven Lawson*
- **Titus For You** *Tim Chester*
- **James For You** *Sam Allberry*
- **1 Peter For You** *Juan Sanchez*

Forthcoming titles include:

- **Micah For You** *Stephen Um*
- **Acts For You (two volumes)** *Al Mohler*
- **1, 2 & 3 John For You** *H.B. Charles Jr.*
- **Revelation For You** *Tim Chester*

Find out more about these resources at:

www.thegoodbook.com/for-you

thegoodbook
COMPANY
Opening up the Bible

At The Good Book Company, we are dedicated to helping Christians and local churches grow. We believe that God's growth process always starts with hearing clearly what he has said to us through his timeless word—the Bible.

Ever since we opened our doors in 1991, we have been striving to produce resources that honor God in the way the Bible is used. We have grown to become an international provider of user-friendly resources to the Christian community, with believers of all backgrounds and denominations using our Bible studies, books, evangelistic resources, DVD-based courses and training events.

We want to equip ordinary Christians to live for Christ day by day, and churches to grow in their knowledge of God, their love for one another, and the effectiveness of their outreach.

Call us for a discussion of your needs or visit one of our local websites for more information on the resources and services we provide.

Your friends at The Good Book Company

NORTH AMERICA
UK & EUROPE
AUSTRALIA
NEW ZEALAND

thegoodbook.com
thegoodbook.co.uk
thegoodbook.com.au
thegoodbook.co.nz

866 244 2165
0333 123 0880
(02) 9564 3555
(+64) 3 343 2463

WWW.CHRISTIANITYEXPLORED.ORG
Our partner site is a great place for those exploring the Christian faith, with a clear explanation of the good news, powerful testimonies and answers to difficult questions.